Psychology and Policing

Policing and Society Series

Series editors: Les Johnston, Frank Leishman, Tim Newburn

Published titles

Policing, Ethics and Human Rights, by Peter Neyroud and Alan Beckley
Policing: a short history, by Philip Rawlings
Policing: an introduction to concepts and practice, by Alan Wright
Psychology and Policing, by Peter B. Ainsworth
Private Policing, by Mark Button

Psychology and Policing

Peter B. Ainsworth

WILLAN
PUBLISHING

Published by

Willan Publishing
Culmcott House
Mill Street, Uffculme
Cullompton, Devon
EX15 3AT, UK
Tel: +44(0)1884 840337
Fax: +44(0)1884 840251
e-mail: info@willanpublishing.co.uk
Website: www.willanpublishing.co.uk

Published simultaneously in the USA and Canada by

Willan Publishing
c/o ISBS, 5824 N.E. Hassalo St
Portland, Oregon 97213-3644, USA
Tel: +001(0)503 287 3093
Fax: +001(0)503 280 8832
Website: www.isbs.com

First published 2002

ISBN 1-903240-45-X (cased)
ISBN 1-903240-44-1 (paper)

British Library Cataloguing-in-Publication Data

A catalogue record for this book is available from the British Library.

Printed by T J International Ltd, Trecerus Industrial Estate, Padstow, Cornwall
Typeset by PDQ Typesetting, Newcastle-under-Lyme, Staffordshire

Contents

List of illustrations

Introduction

The fields of psychology and policing may not, at first glance, appear to make very obvious bedfellows. Whilst the former discipline may be associated in the public's mind with laboratory based experiments, the latter's public image may be more of dangerous work involving the pursuit of menacing criminals. If psychology and policing have one thing in common it is perhaps that each suffers from considerable misunderstanding about what they involve. The public's perception of psychology may indeed be of an individual carrying out experiments in a laboratory, but it may equally be of a Freud-like therapist carrying out psychoanalysis on some unfortunate individual who is struggling to make sense of a feeling of anxiety. Alternatively a more recent image may be of a psychological profiler portrayed in some fictional television series using his supposed powers to help the police 'crack' some difficult case or other. In terms of policing, a member of the public's image may be drawn from seeing police officers dealing with rioting on the streets, or from having recently been stopped for a minor traffic offence.

The point is that both psychology and policing are multifaceted professions, yet images of each are formed often from biased media portrayals or from brief encounters with members of one of the professions. Few members of the public, let alone most police officers, will have come across a psychologist in their day-to-day life and will thus have little idea as to what exactly this discipline has to offer. Some of the stereotypes about each profession are encapsulated by Martin Reisser. Recalling his early experiences as the first ever police psychologist to be appointed in the USA in 1968, Reisser recalls that at that time:

> Police tended to view psychologists as fuzzy-headed, cloud-nine types who had trouble finding the rest room. Psychologists in turn

tended to perceive the police as ham-handed rednecks, brutal, insensitive, and preferring muscle over mind.

(Reisser, 1995: xii)

White and Honig (1995: 258) suggest that police officers and psychologists have often been wary of each other. According to these authors, police officers may have a prejudice against psychologists because of certain areas in which they have come across such individuals. These include:

- Watching 'do-gooder' psychologists testifying on behalf of criminals.

- Dealing with mentally ill individuals who have been inappropriately released back onto the streets by a psychologist.

- Seeing psychologists apparently protecting malingerers within the organisation who appear to be weak officers who are abusing the system.

- Labelling psychologists as 'the enemy' as they have the power to prevent a person from joining the force, or can prevent an officer returning to work if they are deemed to be 'unfit for duty'.

Lest the reader thinks that there is any truth in any of these views, it is perhaps appropriate to consider what psychologists do, or do not do.

The most simple definition of psychology is that it is *The Study of Behaviour*. Many psychologists might prefer to describe their work as the study of *human* behaviour, although a few individuals still spend much of their time studying animals other than humans. This definition is simple but it doesn't really tell us much about how psychologists go about their work. It might be argued that sociologists, social anthropologists and psychiatrists also study human behaviour, yet there are notable differences between these disciplines and psychology.

Psychology likes to consider itself a science and as such often adopts experimental methods similar to those used in other sciences. This is one reason why a great deal of psychological research is carried out within the psychology laboratory, where conditions can be controlled and extraneous variables eliminated. However, some within the profession have argued that the laboratory is not an appropriate place to study the many subtleties and complexities that human behaviour can involve. Nevertheless, psychologists are generally united in their wish to study human behaviour in a systematic, methodical and controlled way. Such study has led to the accumulation of a great deal of knowledge about many of the factors that underlie human behaviour, although, as with any relatively new discipline, much more remains to be uncovered.

But psychology has now become more than the simple *study* of human behaviour. The knowledge that has been accumulated has enabled professionals to work with individuals and organisations and to apply the results of the work. Thus in the field of education, educational psychologists can help to identify the reasons why individual children may be experiencing difficulties and to offer help to both the individual and the school. Clinical psychologists can also use their knowledge base to help those suffering from behavioural problems or mental illness to tackle their difficulties more effectively. Organisational psychologists can also work towards improving the functioning of large companies and by so doing improve the welfare of employees.

In all of these examples, psychologists are able to use an accumulated knowledge to understand people and, hopefully to help them. But what has all this to do with policing? It will be argued throughout this book that policing is also about understanding and dealing with people. Whilst the fictional portrayals of police work shown on our television screens may have us believe that police work is an 'all action' job with danger lurking around every street corner, the reality is that most tasks performed by police officers involve simple interactions with members of the public. Yet comparatively little training time is devoted to teaching police officers how to deal with such encounters successfully and professionally. A police officer who has to convey news of a sudden death to a distraught relative may have little training in how this might be carried out in the most empathetic way and instead may fall back on intuition or 'advice' offered by colleagues in the police canteen. Learning how to deal sympathetically with victims of crime may not come high on a list of training priorities yet such an ability will have a profound effect on victims' perceptions of the police.

If psychology has tried to adopt a systematic method of accumulating knowledge, policing has not always done so. It has been said that much of police training is anecdote driven. Police officers tend to use methods that have proved to be successful in the past and training is offered by 'insiders' who pass on the knowledge that they have gained on the job. Only relatively recently have there been systematic attempts to test out what works and what does not work in policing. The introduction of performance indicators and concepts such as policing by objectives has compelled police forces to examine what they are doing and how they are doing it. However, there remains a belief that the solution to most problems can be found within the organisation rather than as a result of knowledge accumulated by social scientists outside. Whilst there have been a number of important initiatives that have brought psychology to the task of policing (Ainsworth, 1995) the full potential of the discipline has not been fully recognised by the majority of people working within the filed of law enforcement. Even where initiatives have been accepted and adopted, they have not always been embraced by officers working at grass roots level (Clarke and Milne, 2001).

This book will look at some of the ways in which psychology and policing are, or perhaps should be, related. It is more than a simple review of what has become known as 'police psychology'. (The interested reader may wish to consult sources such as Blau (1994) and Kurke and Scrivner (1995) for a review of traditional police psychology.) This book will consider a number of areas in which knowledge accumulated by psychologists will be of value to police officers in their day to day work. But it will also provide some examples of the way in which psychology can fruitfully be applied to many everyday policing situations. Whilst a great deal of psychological research is concerned with the generation of theories and the testing of hypotheses, a great deal of effort is also expended on the application of theory to practice. It is the latter activity that will be the main focus of this volume. The book is divided up as follows.

Chapter 1, *Person Perception and Interpersonal Skills*, looks at how we perceive the social world and considers some of the skills needed for successful social interaction. Chapter 2, *Attribution, Prejudice and Stereotyping*, examines the way in which we attribute causes for behaviour and considers what an important role prejudice and stereotyping can play in much everyday interaction.

Chapter 3, *Recruitment, Selection and Training*, considers how psychology may be able to help in the recruitment and training of police officers. Psychometric testing has developed rapidly in recent years although, as we will see in this chapter, the development and use of appropriate tests is not always straightforward. Chapter 4, *Aggression and Violence*, examines some of the more common theories that have been developed to explain these forms of behaviour and also considers how police officers might deal with violent incidents and individuals.

Chapter 5, *Perception and Memory*, examines how the psychological research in these two areas offers an explanation of the processes that might differ from that of the layperson. The chapter will also consider whether procedures such as identification parades might lead to problems and difficulties. Chapter 6, *Retrieving Information*, considers how police officers might best recover information from witnesses and victims. This is an area in which there have been important recent advances, in particular with the development of the cognitive interview technique.

Chapter 7, *Interviewing Suspects*, looks at appropriate and inappropriate strategies that police officers might use when interviewing those suspected of having committed an offence. The chapter will also consider the detection of deception and the thorny question of false confessions. Chapter 8, *Stress and Policing*, will examine the concept of stress in general and look at some of the ways in which police officers might encounter and deal with stressful situations.

Chapter 9, *Crime Patterns and Offender Profiling*, looks at a number of recent developments in this emerging area and assesses the usefulness of profiling in everyday police work. Chapter 10, *Hostage Taking and Negotiation*, examines how police officers might best deal with scenarios in which negotiation is necessary. The chapter draws on some important psychological principles that can be used, especially in situations in which hostages are involved. Finally, in the Conclusion an attempt will be made to pull together the various strands and themes that have been introduced throughout the book and to assess the future prospects in terms of psychology and policing.

Chapter 1

Person perception and interpersonal skills

In the introduction to this volume it was suggested that a great deal of everyday police work involves simple interactions with others. Social interaction is a subject that has been studied closely by psychologists and a great deal of insight has been offered by the research in this area. At a time when the police service is increasingly concerned about its public image, it seems appropriate that police officers should know something about how humans perceive, and are perceived by, others. Forming an impression of another person and interacting successfully with another individual are core social skills that are essential in our daily life. Understanding such processes enables us to make sense of other people and to interpret their behaviour correctly. However, understanding these processes also enables us to control to some extent the impression that others form of us. One slovenly dressed, gum-chewing, slouching, rude police officer may do a great deal of harm to a police force that is trying to improve its public image. In this chapter we will draw upon a range of research from both social and cognitive psychology and attempt to relate the findings to the context of policing.

Impression formation

Whenever an individual meets someone for the first time they tend to form an immediate impression of that person. They may attend to a number of different factors but will generally be drawn to a few key or salient features. They may initially attend to the person's face in an effort to form some impression of the sort of person with whom they are dealing.

Facial appearance

The person's face will tend to give them some clues as to the person's sex, their race and their age. However, most perceivers will also go beyond this basic information and try to assess aspects of the other person's personality or character from their facial appearance. Police officers may believe that they have more skill than most in differentiating between an 'honest' and a 'dishonest' face, although as we will see later in this volume, such presumptions may be ill founded.

The accurate judgement of personality from an individual's appearance is actually quite difficult. Despite this, people do often form an opinion of another's traits based on their outward appearance or upon a small sample of their behaviour. Whilst people may be able to detect traits such as extroversion or warmth from a brief exposure, other aspects of personality (e.g. honesty and conscientiousness) appear more difficult to detect accurately (Park and Krauss, 1992). Traits such as honesty are quite difficult to define accurately and this may be one reason why our perception of this trait is difficult. For example a man may be said to be 'honest' in the sense that he has never been convicted of a crime yet he regularly uses the office phone to make private calls and often takes home quantities of his company's office supplies. Even if people are able to assess certain aspects of personality accurately this may not in itself be particularly useful. While many aspects of personality are linked to the way in which people behave, knowledge of a person's personality rarely allows us to make accurate predictions as to their future behaviour. Thus even if we were able to establish that a person was basically dishonest, this would not allow us to say when or where they are likely to steal next.

Although humans do tend to observe the face closely on first encounter, the impression that is formed may not necessarily be accurate. Whilst clues as to an individual's race, sex and age are very useful, presumptions as to a person's likely character and personality may be less easily gleaned from the simple observation of a person's facial features. Although people can use make-up or cosmetic surgery in order to modify their facial appearance, to a large extent people are stuck with the face with which they are born. Thus, somewhat paradoxically, the aspect of the individual over which they have arguably the least control (i.e. their facial appearance) is the one which is most often used as the basis of a first impression. Expressions such as 'His face doesn't fit' or 'I didn't like the look of him' are used to suggest that there is a certain type of face that fits well and is acceptable in certain environments and another type that does not. Some job application forms may perpetuate such a view by asking that applicants submit a recent photograph of

7

themselves along with their application form. One might presume that those making such requests believe that the photographic information will help them to decide what sort of person the applicant is. Alternatively, one might suspect that the provision of a photograph allows some screening of applicants on the basis of race or some other obvious dimension.

The reason why face perception might be important is that it allows people to make an initial classification of the individual they have just met. Knowing that we are talking to a young white male may produce a different set of behaviours than knowing that we are talking to an elderly black female. To some extent this classification leads people to employ stereotypes, a subject that will be covered more fully in Chapter 2. It would appear that the categorisation of other people is important as it can save a great deal of time and effort when interacting with others. If humans had to ask every individual whom they meet what they are like before they attempted an interaction, the world would become a very difficult place. For this reason the tendency is for a brief observation to be followed by a classification of the individual along a number of dimensions. The face is by no means the only clue to which people attend when making such classifications but it does allow for an initial sifting.

While some faces may evoke a fairly neutral response, others may trigger a much more acute reaction. For example a particularly attractive face may arouse much more interest than would one that is deemed to be only moderately attractive. Similarly a particularly ugly or disfigured face will tend to command a great deal more attention than one that is simply 'average'. Bull and McAlpine (1998) suggest that people often have a view as to what facial features certain types of criminal may typically possess. Such a belief may have an effect on jurors when they are trying to decide upon the guilt or innocence of an accused person. We will return to this issue in the next chapter.

Hairstyles and clothing

Perhaps next on the list of features to which people attend would come hair and clothes. Hair is much more easily altered than are facial features, and so to some extent hair style and even hair colour can be manipulated in such a way that the individual has some control over the sort of signals that are given off. Perhaps surprisingly there has been relatively little psychological research into the effects of hairstyle, length and colour on person perception and impression formation. One possible reason is that the perception of hairstyle is to some extent culture, or even sub-culture dependent. Very long or very short hair may give off different signals in different cultures or at different points in time. In the 1980s, 'Skinheads' were invariably perceived in Britain as troublemakers, yet in 2001 such short hairstyles were perceived as fashionable and worn by many professional footballers. In most Western police forces, long hair and beards are frowned upon, presumably because it is felt that they will give off the 'wrong' message.

Physique

Physique is another cue to which people attend when meeting someone for the first time. There is a something of a stereotype with regard to physique. Many believe that thin people are nervous, fat people are jolly and muscular people are aggressive. Whether such stereotypes are valid is a moot point, but the very fact that people may respond to body shape in such a way is in itself interesting. Some early research (Glueck and Glueck, 1956) suggested that there might be a link between criminality and body shape, in that those with strong muscular physiques were thought more likely to be found amongst the criminal fraternity. Although such theories have now been questioned they do raise an interesting point in relation to cause and effect. For example, it may be the case that those with a strong physique and an intimidating presence are sought out by other criminals and persuaded to join their gangs. On the other hand any young male who wishes to indulge in a life of violent crime may decide to spend hours working out in the gym and even take anabolic steroids in order to enhance his physique.

Voice and speech style

Although many of these visual clues are important, humans also tend to pay close attention to what a person says and to how they say it. Impressions can be formed on the basis of the softness or hardness of a person's voice, the accent that they have acquired and the speed with which they speak. Certain speech impediments such as lisps will tend to have a significant effect on the way in which a speaker is perceived. Language is said to be one of the main factors that separates humans from the rest of the animal kingdom and this may be one reason why person perception can be affected by differences in voice or speech. A person who speaks very slowly or in a very high pitched voice will be perceived somewhat differently than one who speaks with a more normal speed and pitch.

Forming an instant impression

We can see that many static features will affect both how we perceive and are perceived by others. Many of these signals may be obvious ones yet people rarely stop to think how they have formed a particular impression of a certain individual. It is not uncommon for someone to take an 'instant dislike' to a person they have just met, or, at the other extreme, to talk of 'love at first sight'. Police officers on patrol may decide that they do not 'like the look of' an individual whom they encounter and choose to stop and question him whilst allowing other people to go on their way unchallenged. Police officers may even brag about the fact that they can spot someone who appears to be in some way suspicious and, as a result, make an arrest. If police officers possess such skills and are invariably right in their hunches, then we should perhaps admire and applaud them. However, if such hunches come about as a result of prejudice and stereotyping then it is a cause for concern. We will return to this notion in Chapter 2; however, it is perhaps appropriate at this point to draw attention to the dangers of a self-fulfilling prophecy.

If police officers believe that they are able to identify the sort of individual who is likely to be carrying a weapon or who is likely to be in possession of illegal drugs they will tend to stop only those individuals who match this template or 'schema' (see Chapter 5). The gun-carrying drug dealer whose physical appearance and demographic characteristics do not match the template will of course go unchallenged, and as result the officer may never feel a need to revise the template in the future. The officer may even feel vindicated by the fact that the person who was stopped was in possession of a weapon or drugs and was subsequently convicted of a criminal offence. But such a 'result' may do little to encourage the officer to look for other dangerous individuals whose physical appearance is different from that of the majority of people who are stopped and searched.

If a white Metropolitan Police officer working in Brixton believes that Afro-Caribbean youths are responsible for the majority of crime in the local area, the officer will be more likely to stop and question such people when out on patrol. Indeed it may be found that in an average tour of duty, the officer stops and questions five black youths and one white. Even if only 5% of those stopped are found to have committed an offence, the figures at the end of the year might appear to justify the officer's actions. But it may be that 5% of white youths who are stopped might also have committed an offence. Yet the fact that the officer stops five times as many black youths as white will go some way towards explaining the apparently racial difference that might appear in the official figures published at the end of the year. As we will see in Chapter 2, stereotypes can have a powerful effect on the way in which people perceive and interact with the world.

Non-verbal communication (NVC)

So far in this chapter we have looked at a number of static variables that affect how people perceive others. Whilst factors such as physical appearance can be very important in the early stages of interpersonal perception, it is often by interacting with the individual that a better image of what the person is really like may begin to emerge. Although people tend to listen closely to what someone is saying, they will also be taking in information that is provided non-verbally. A police officer may for example pay close attention to the non-verbal signals that a person gives off as the officer approaches them on the street. When questioned, the suspect may well deny any wrongdoing but the officer may be justified in examining other signals that are being given off whilst the denial is being made. Although as we noted above the officer may use age and race as early filtering devices when deciding who to stop on the street, non-verbal cues may also alert the officer that the person appears to have something to hide. Even an individual's posture when standing on the street corner may lead the officer to believe that they have little respect for authority and are worth speaking to.

Psychologists have carried out a great deal of research on non-verbal communication and its role in interaction. We will now consider some of this and assess its relevance for police officers.

Gestures

Gestures are often used as a way of illustrating certain aspects of speech or, in some cases, as alternatives to speech. An officer may for example point directly at the individual who he/she wishes to question and such a gesture may reinforce an instruction to the person that they should come over and speak to the officer. Rude gestures such as giving someone the finger can also be used as effective forms of communication when speech is perhaps difficult. Gestures can thus be used both as speech illustrators and also as speech substitutes. Some individuals use gestures a great deal whilst others may use them less frequently. It would also appear that some cultures use gestures much more frequently than do others. For example British communicators tend to use their hands much less often than say Italians. For some cultures touching the other person whilst talking is seen as quite normal whilst in other cultures such gestures would be frowned upon. It is important that police officers are aware that there are such cultural differences. Variations in these norms can mean that an officer might inadvertently offend a member of the public by the inappropriate use of a certain gesture. And similarly the officer may misinterpret a gesture used by someone from a different culture and, as a result, form an inappropriate impression of the person.

Gestures might also be examined closely to see whether they may be a clue as to how an individual is feeling. For example, an individual who wrings his hands or tugs his earlobe when denying involvement in a crime may be perceived as experiencing stress. In some cases this stress may be presumed by the police officer to emanate from the person's guilt and fear of being found out. However, as we shall see in Chapter 7, assumptions about the truthfulness or otherwise of a suspect's statements may not always be accurate. Having said that, a change in the use of gestures may signal that some change has occurred within the individual. For example an individual who suddenly stops using hand gestures or even sits on their hands may be doing so because of some change in the way that they are feeling. Where clues are picked up by an interviewer, it is often because a person's use of gestures changes at some point. It is much more difficult to interpret gestures accurately when there is no such baseline from which to work.

Posture

We made reference to posture earlier in the chapter. Observation of a person's posture can be used in order to try to understand how the person may be feeling or, in some cases what sort of person the other appears to be. If someone has just completed a very tiring or difficult task they may collapse into a chair and sprawl themselves out with their head lolling. Anyone who sees the person positioned this way may have little problem in interpreting what the other person is feeling. But posture can also be used in more subtle ways. For example a person who leans forward intently when another is speaking may be suggesting that they really are interested in what the other has to say. By contrast the person who slouches in the chair and rarely makes eye contact may be suggesting to the other that they are totally uninterested.

In some cases, posture can be manipulated deliberately so as to give off a certain image or signal, but in other cases the change in posture may be inadvertent. For example, a police officer who is interviewing a suspect may suddenly become much more interested in something that is being said and may pay closer attention to the speaker. In doing so the interviewer's posture may change completely. We use expressions such as 'my ear's pricked up when he said...'. Such statements are not meant literally but more to provide an example of how our increased interest in another person's story may lead to some change in posture.

One aspect of NVC that is related to posture is the notion of interpersonal distance. How we choose to stand or sit when interacting with another is important, but equally important is the distance at which we position ourselves. People require a certain level of personal space in order to feel comfortable, but there are also culturally defined norms of interpersonal distance (Sommer, 1969). These norms are based upon the type of encounter that two people are having. If two good friends are having an amiable chat they will tend to sit or stand quite close together. They may even choose to touch each other on occasions. On the other hand if two people meet for the first time, especially if it is in a tense or formal situation, they will tend to interact at a much greater interpersonal distance. On some occasions these types of behaviour are indicative of the form of the interaction, but they may also be perceived as indicators of the sort of person who is being observed. We may for example describe one person as 'touchy-feely' or another as 'stand-offish'. It is easy to see the derivation of such expressions.

One occasion upon which norms of interpersonal space are broken is when a police officer has to arrest someone. In order to do this the officer will need to invade the other's personal space, an act that may in itself lead to the other person becoming uncomfortable or perhaps aggressive (see Chapter 4). Invasion of personal space can also be used as a way of threatening another individual. A police officer who deliberately stands or sits very close to a suspect when carrying out an interview may succeed in intimidating the person. Indeed one book dealing with interrogations and confessions (Inbau and Reid, 1963) advocates that an officer should 'move his chair in closer so that ultimately one of the subject's knees is just about in between the interrogator's two knees'. Such tactics would appear to be inappropriate in a situation in which the purpose of the interview is, supposedly, to establish the facts in a case (see Chapter 7).

Eye contact and other speech regulators

Speech is one thing that separates humans from the rest of the animal kingdom and allows a great deal of communication to take place. Yet the power of speech does not in itself guarantee a successful interaction between two individuals. For a successful and rewarding conversation to take place, the exchange needs to be managed successfully. For example it is important that two people do not both try to speak at the same time or that one 'knows' when the other person is inviting them to respond. Whilst there are a number of ways in which speech is regulated, eye contact is perhaps the most important. A person who regularly looks at the other while they are speaking, especially if such glances are accompanied by head nods or smiles, will encourage the other person to carry on speaking and suggest that the listener is interested in what is being said. The person speaking may also check regularly that the other is listening by making eye contact. The person may signal the point at which they would like the other person to start speaking by looking up at the other in a more prolonged stare.

As with many other aspects of non-verbal communication we are often unaware of their importance until someone breaks the (unwritten) rules. A person who stares at us coldly and unflinchingly may make us feel self conscious and uncomfortable. By contrast a person who refuses to make any eye contact at all during a conversation will tend to be perceived as odd or cold. When faced with such an individual we will generally try to curtail a conversation quickly. In general, the more that another person makes eye contact with us, the more we will tend to like them. However, there are some notable exceptions to this tendency.

Levels of intimacy are often obvious by the amount of eye contact that two people make. People in love may (literally) stare into each other's eyes for hours, whereas a couple who are about to split up may hardly make eye contact at all during a conversation. However, eye contact can also be used not as an indicator of intimacy but as a threat gesture. One person who is challenging another to a fight may stare at the other person for a long period. If the other person looks away quite quickly the aggressor may feel that they already have the upper hand as the person has indicated submission by looking away. In the animal kingdom, a lowering of the eyes often indicates submission.

Another point about eye contact is that it is an important way of communicating both interest and intention. A police officer who wishes to communicate effectively with a member of the public needs to be aware of the signals that they are giving off through their level of eye contact. Eye contact can be used as a way of checking that the other person is attending to and understanding what is being said. But it can also be used as a way of expressing interest in the other person and what they are saying. Police officers who insist on wearing mirrored sunglasses whilst talking to a member of the public are unlikely to experience an easy conversational exchange.

Whilst eye contact is very important it must be recognised that there are cultural variations in what is regarded as the norm. In some societies a great deal of eye contact is expected and encouraged, while in others much less eye contact will tend to be used. This is an important point to bear in mind especially in situations where there are cultural differences in the background of the two people engaged in a conversation. It would be all too easy for a white police officer to presume that an ethnic minority individual's refusal to make eye contact is a signal that they have something to hide In this case, the refusal to make eye contact may be simply a normal piece of behaviour for someone from such a background. We will see in Chapter 7 that the stereotypical view that someone who refuses to make eye contact is lying is simplistic and in many cases grossly inaccurate. However, as we noted in respect of other aspects of non-verbal communication, it is easier to interpret such information accurately when we have a baseline of 'normal' behaviour with which to compare the current conduct.

The relationship between verbal and non-verbal communication

In most cases non-verbal communication is used in addition to verbal communication as a way of helping along the conversational exchange. As we noted earlier, conversations in which there is no eye contact tend to be more stilted than those in which there is a normal amount of gaze. In most cases the non-verbal behaviour supports and confirms what is being said. However, in some cases the non-verbal communication may be at odds with the words being used. One obvious example is in the use of sarcasm. If a friend tells us that we are looking particularly smart but says this with a barely hidden mocking smirk, we may reasonably presume that the friend actually means the opposite of what the words might suggest. If someone yawns all the time that we are speaking yet assures us that they really are interested in what is being said, we would probably tend not to believe them.

Non-verbal communication can be an important source of information about another's emotions. Large numbers of movements, especially where one part of the body does something to another (e.g. scratching, rubbing, biting nails) suggest a degree of emotional arousal – the greater the frequency of such behaviours, the higher the level of arousal (Baron and Byrne, 2000: 42). However, as we noted above, knowing that someone is becoming more aroused does not prove that they are lying. We should also bear in mind that some people are intrinsically more 'nervous' than others. For this reason we cannot assume that a certain level of non-verbal communication indicates the same thing in different individuals. Stage actors can quickly become adept at communicating how their character is supposed to be feeling by adopting certain body postures and using certain gestures. But they can also communicate what sort of a person the character is supposed to be by their non-verbal behaviour.

There may be other instances where we get a feeling that what someone is telling us may not truly reflect how they feel about something. In some instances the suspicion may be aroused by the fact that the person's non-verbal behaviour is at odds with what is being said. One obvious example would be where an individual denies verbally something of which they are being accused, yet nods their head throughout the denial. Whilst some of these mismatches may be quite obvious, in other cases they may only be noticed by someone with a detailed knowledge of the many aspects of non-verbal communication. As we will see in Chapter 5, humans have a limited capacity to process incoming information, and, as a result may miss many of the more subtle clues given off during an interaction. However, a police officer whose entire body language signals disinterest to the distraught crime victim will do little to enhance the public perception of the police.

Taylor *et al* (2000: 63) suggest that there are six general principles that govern impression formation. These can be summarised as follows:

- People form an impression of others quickly on the basis of small amounts of information. Having done this people tend then to impute general traits to the individual.

- When viewing another person, observers tend to pay particular attention to the most obvious or salient features of the individual rather than to every single aspect. Details that are particularly distinctive or unusual will be attended to the most.

- Processing information about other individuals involves trying to make sense of their behaviour within its context.

- People tend to organise perceptual information by categorising or grouping information. Thus one of the first things that we do when encountering another person is to place them within the group or category to which we believe they belong. Thus a police officer may be seen as simply a member of the police service rather than having obvious individual qualities that make him/her different from all other police officers.

- People use their existing views of the world to try to interpret or make sense of others' behaviour. Once an individual has been identified as a local criminal we may use the information that we already have about such people so as to interpret the behaviour of the person whom we have just met.

- Our own needs and personal goals will influence how we perceive others. If, for example, we are looking for a person with whom to start a new relationship we may perceive a new acquaintance differently than if we believe we will simply have to work with this other person in the future.

Some of these points will be expanded upon in the next chapter.

Summary

In this chapter we have looked at some important aspects of impression formation and person perception and their possible relevance to policing. Person perception is perhaps best seen as an *inferential* process. In general people observe the appearance and behaviour of another person and infer things about that individual on the basis of this information. If our observations are complete and objective in all cases, this will not necessarily be a problem. However, as we will see in the next chapter, many aspects of person perception rely upon stereotypes and prejudice. As a result we are constantly in danger of misperceiving both people and events in the world.

We have also seen that in many cases non-verbal communication is an important aspect of interaction. Whilst humans rely heavily on the spoken word in order to communicate effectively, non-verbal aspects can be equally, and in some cases more, important. For this reason police officers should be aware of the messages given off by themselves and others.

Further reading

Baron, R. A. and Byrne, D. (2000) *Social Psychology* (9th ed). Boston: Allyn & Bacon; Chapters 2 and 3.
Zebrowitz, L. A. (1997) *Reading Faces*. Boulder CO: Westview Press.

Chapter 2

Attribution, prejudice and stereotyping

In the previous chapter we looked at some of the ways in which people take in and process information about other people. The point was made that humans often try to place each new person whom they encounter into some pre-existing category or group. Categorising others in this way allows people to take shortcuts in the process of finding out something about the other person. Thus recognising that a person is male, middle-aged and a scientist allows us to draw upon information that we already possess about males, middle-aged people and scientists. Placing people into such categories can be useful as it negates the need to ask each new person we meet a large number of questions. Having categorised someone, people will tend to react to the other person in stereotypical ways, based upon their pre-existing knowledge. If such 'knowledge' is accurate and complete this may not necessarily be a problem. However, if such information is inaccurate it will mean that the new person encountered may be evaluated inappropriately. In this chapter we will consider how stereotyping and prejudice can affect all our interactions with others and also affect the attributions that we make about why people behave as they do. We start with a consideration of the attribution process itself.

Attribution

Attribution refers to the way in which people attribute a cause to any particular piece of behaviour. As such it is concerned with the explanation that people give for the behaviour of others, or, in some cases their own behaviour. There has been a great deal of psychological research on attribution in recent years. Knowing how people explain things that happen in their world can give us valuable insights into their thinking and their social functioning.

Many studies of attribution are based on the belief that people are naturally curious. There is an assumption that people want to know why things happen in the world and why people behave as they do. In the same way that psychologists study and then try to explain human behaviour, the non-psychologist will also look at examples of human behaviour and try to work out why they occurred. In general the more unusual or striking the event or behaviour, the more time and effort people will expend in trying to piece together an explanation. However, unlike the psychologist, the ordinary person may do this in a somewhat unsophisticated and possibly biased way. As a result they may reach a conclusion that is naïve or simply inaccurate. Towards the end of this section we will look at some of the biases that can affect the attribution process and can explain some of the errors that people can make.

The attribution process may perhaps be best illustrated by considering an example. Suppose a police officer is patrolling when he/she notices a youth acting suspiciously. The officer walks over to speak to the youth but as he/she does so the youth runs away and is never caught. How might the officer explain such an occurrence? In searching for an explanation the officer might consider a number of possibilities. For example it may be concluded that the youth is a bad person who is fearful of the police. On the other hand the officer might conclude that although the youth is not necessarily a bad person themself they were doing something wrong at that point in time and ran away rather than risk being arrested by the officer.

These two explanations have one important difference. In the first one, the officer makes the assumption that the youth behaved the way that they did because they are just 'that sort of person'. In other words, the explanation for the behaviour lies within the youth themself rather than in the particular circumstances that appertained at the time that they ran away. In the second explanation the officer is seeking to explain the behaviour more in terms of the situational factors that were present at the time of the behaviour. In this example it might be interesting to try to establish why the officer reached the conclusion that he/she did. For example, if the youth was female and white, would there be a tendency to reach a different conclusion than if they were male and black?

Internal vs. external attributions

This distinction between explanations that lie within the individual and those that lie outside is a crucial one. Psychologists refer to this process as making an *internal* or an *external* attribution. This distinction is also sometimes referred to as *dispositional* vs. *situational* attributions. Individuals are more likely to be thought to be responsible for their actions if an internal attribution is made, whereas they are less likely to be 'blamed' if the observer believes that there were situational factors that more readily explain the behaviour. Let us consider another example. A police officer observes a man driving a car at almost twice the speed limit and decides he/she should stop the car and report the driver. The police officer might believe that the driver is clearly a 'bad' person who has no respect for other road users and needs to be taught a lesson. In other words the officer would make an *internal* or *dispositional* attribution when trying to understand this particular piece of behaviour. However, on stopping the vehicle the distraught motorist explains to the officer that he has just had a phone call from the local hospital to say that his only child has been involved in an accident and is critically ill. In such circumstances, the officer may revise the original hypothesis about the man's driving and instead offer a situational explanation. The officer may conclude that, in such circumstances, he/she may well have done the same thing and that it would be inappropriate to add to the man's problems by reporting the speeding offence.

The distinction between internal and external attributions is an important one. As noted earlier, a person will be presumed to be more responsible for his/her actions if an internal attribution is made. By contrast, if an external attribution is made, responsibility for the action may be deemed to lie outside the individual. Thus a youth who joins a local gang and daubs graffiti on a number of buildings might be presumed by the local police to be 'just that sort of person'. However if the youth's mother is made aware of his behaviour she may explain it by saying 'He's a good lad really but he just got in with the wrong crowd'. Such an attempt to offer a situational explanation is perhaps understandable given parents' tendency to protect their offspring.

When a court is trying to decide what sentence is appropriate for a particular offender it may try to establish whether an internal or external attribution is more pertinent. On some occasions the court may ask that pre-sentence reports or psychiatric evaluations be produced. These will give some background information about the offender, their circumstances and perhaps their motives for committing a particular offence. If, for example, the case is one in which a woman has killed her husband, the fact that she suffered serious physical abuse for many years may be taken into account and a light sentence be handed down. In such a case the court would appear to be taking the view that an external attribution is appropriate. The fact that the woman had suffered for years at the hands of her violent partner is a 'better' explanation than one that suggests she is a violent and dangerous person from whom the public must be protected.

Other attributions

There are other dimensions along which attributions may vary including those of *stability/instability* and *controllability/uncontrollability*. In the case of the *stability/instability* dimension, an assessment might be made of whether the type of behaviour that a person has exhibited is a representative example of their normal behaviour, i.e. is it something consistent or stable. For this reason someone who commits an offence that appears to be 'out of character' may be judged less harshly than one whose latest criminal act appears to be part of a consistent pattern of deviant conduct. Most people may be capable of committing dreadful acts given a particular set of circumstances or sufficient provocation. However, in some cases the horrendous act may be judged to be an 'unstable' example of the person's behaviour and thus one that is unlikely to be repeated, providing the same set of circumstances do not recur.

During times of war soldiers may commit dreadful atrocities yet their actions are often judged as 'understandable' given the situations in which they found themselves. Most soldiers do not return to civilian life having been branded as homicidal maniacs. Although they may have killed many people in combat, society tends to form the judgement that their killing was due to a particular and perhaps unique set of circumstances and is not a reflection of the sort of person they really are. When judging and making attributions about the actions of others, people adopt what Kelly calls the *covariation* principle (Kelly, 1967). The covariation principle suggests that people look for consistent patterns in others' behaviour – they try to establish whether a particular effect and a particular cause are found together across a range of different situations. Considering the example of the soldier, an observer may realise that the killing of other people is not a consistent pattern of behaviour but one that is specific to the war situation. In other words killing other people covaries with being in the army and going to war but not to other more normal situations.

In relation to the *controllability/uncontrollability* dimension, people tend to form a judgement as to whether a person's actions were or were not under their own control. Returning to the example of the soldiers in wartime, observers may form the view that their actions were largely beyond their own personal control and that they were 'simply obeying orders'. The female police officer who arrests large numbers of men for kerb-crawling may be doing so not because she has a desire to see men who use prostitutes punished, but because her senior officer has commanded her to take this course of action.

If someone is asked to account for their misbehaviour they may claim that 'it was just an accident' and thus outside their control. A motorist may try to claim that the collision with the car in front occurred because the brakes locked and the car skidded, rather than admit that they were following too closely. In the former case the motorist is claiming that he/she had 'no control' over what happened but in the latter the motorist would have to admit that they could have avoided the collision if they had driven differently. The youth charged with causing criminal damage may claim that, at the time of the offence, he was very drunk and did not really know what he was doing. Despite the fact that alcohol appears to play a part in a large number of criminal offences, courts rarely accept that the offender's intoxication should be seen as an 'excuse' for their behaviour. This is interesting in that most people would admit that they do things when they are drunk that they would not consider doing when sober. Presumably courts take the view that, whilst the inebriation might mean that the person had less control of their actions, they *chose* to drink rather than to stay sober. By offering this reasoning the court can argue that the person should accept responsibility for their actions as they did have some degree of 'control'.

When growing up, children seem to learn quickly that they might escape serious punishment for breaking household objects if they claim that it was an accident and not really their fault at all. Parents may of course counter this argument by pointing out that if only the child had been more careful the 'accident' would not have occurred. Nevertheless children learn at an early age that making an external attribution for their own bad deeds is usually a good idea.

In extreme cases a court may form a judgement that an individual should not be held responsible for their actions because they are insane (and thus, presumably, unable to control their behaviour). In such cases a court would tend to recommend psychiatric 'treatment' rather than 'punishment'. Today, those accused of murder may claim that whilst they are not actually insane, they did not, at least at the time of the offence, have total control over their actions. In such cases the court may judge that they had 'diminished responsibility' and should thus be convicted of manslaughter rather than murder (Peay, 1997). This is an important distinction because those convicted of murder in Britain must receive a mandatory sentence of life imprisonment. By contrast those convicted of manslaughter are eligible for a diverse range of punishments including community service and probation.

Consideration of these attributional dimensions offers some explanation as to why people form the judgements that they do when considering others' behaviour. Attributing causes to events in the world and establishing the reasons why people act as they do satisfies what appears to be a natural curiosity about the world around us. Heider (1958) suggests that people act like 'naïve psychologists' when trying to make sense of events and actions. They may develop beliefs about other people based not on careful study and experimentation but rather by their experience with the world. However, problems can arise when people make inappropriate and inaccurate attributions about the actions of other people. We will see later in the chapter how prejudice and stereotyping will affect attributions, but for now we will consider some biases that can occur in the attribution process.

Errors in attribution

We noted earlier in this chapter that one of the main distinctions that people make when attributing causes to behaviour is between explanations that lie within the individual (e.g. their disposition or personality) and those that lie outside (e.g. the situational pressures). If such attributions are accurate then we may have little cause to be concerned. However, psychological research has suggested that there is a consistent bias that occurs when people are making internal or external attributions. So pervasive is this tendency that it has been labelled the *fundamental attribution error* (Ross, 1977).

The so-called 'error' refers to the fact that when people are seeking explanations for the behaviour of others they consistently over-estimate the influence of internal factors and under-estimate the influence of external factors. Thus people are more likely to 'blame' others when explaining behaviours that have had bad consequences for another person and less likely to recognise the factors external to the individual that may explain the unfortunate incident. Thus if we see an old man fall from his pedal cycle we will be inclined to presume that he is the 'master of his own misfortune' and fell off because he is just a careless or clumsy person. In making such an attribution we may tend to overlook the situational factors that might have contributed to the poor man's misfortune. We may not even realise that the road is very slippery at the point where the man fell or that his bike suffered a sudden puncture just before the accident.

This tendency to play down situational factors and to over-emphasise dispositional ones was illustrated in one experiment carried out by Ross (1977). In this study, Ross had pairs of people take part in what was said to be a general knowledge test. One member of each pair was asked to think up a number of general knowledge questions and the other was invited to try to answer the questions. Other people were then asked to observe the question and answer sessions and to make attributions about the intellectual abilities of the questioner and the person being questioned. Ross found that people consistently rated the questioner as being more intelligent than the person being questioned. This presumption is perhaps understandable given that one person appeared to (literally) know all the answers while the other person did not.

However, in making this assessment it appeared that the observers consistently under-estimated the situational factors that appertained in this case. Obviously the person who made up the quiz would only choose questions to which he already knew the answers. There would inevitably be some questions to which the other person did not know the answer, but this was simply a facet of the way in which the question and answer sessions were set up. (Of course if the roles were then reversed, the new question setter would then have an advantage.) This factor was seemingly ignored by those who consistently judged the questioner to be more intelligent.

This tendency to attribute dispositional qualities to the behaviour of others appears to occur almost spontaneously and even without awareness. Gilbert *et al* (1992) suggest that the use of information about the situational context of behaviour may be part of a secondary and more complex process that would involve a reconsideration of the original position. However, these researchers suggest that in many cases people simply do not bother to consider factors that might challenge their original assumption. This is particularly likely when they are busy with other tasks.

Although the fundamental attribution error is well documented in the psychological literature, at least one researcher has suggested that it might be much more likely to be found in Western cultures. Miller (1984) carried out some research that suggested that in Hindu communities, people are more likely to offer situational rather than dispositional explanations when asked to judge others' behaviour. Despite this, the fundamental attribution error can have important consequences for many aspects of law enforcement. For example, police officers who stop motorists for a minor traffic offence may be less likely to simply caution the offender if they believe that the person's behaviour was due to internal rather than external factors. Police officers interviewing crime victims may also be less sympathetic to their plight if they believe, perhaps inappropriately, that the victim should bear some of the responsibility for what happened.

There are a number of other interesting errors or biases that have been found to occur in attribution research. One of these is the so-called *actor-observer* bias. This refers to the fact that whilst we may tend to attribute others' behaviour to dispositional factors, we often seek to explain our own behaviour by reference to situational forces. Thus if it is we who fall from the pedal cycle rather the old man referred to in the example above, we may start an active search for some external factor onto which we can place the blame.

There are a number of possible explanations as to why this actor-observer bias occurs. One relates to the fact that actors and observers have access to different kinds of information. In the case of our own behaviour we have a history upon which we can draw in seeking an appropriate explanation. Thus if we have been riding a pedal cycle for 20 years and never before fallen off, we may presume that on this occasion there were some unusual situational characteristics that caused the fall. By comparison, the observer of the old man falling from the cycle has only that one example of his behaviour from which to judge. Similarly if we observe someone being stopped for speeding we may presume that their speeding behaviour on this occasion is a reflection of the way that they normally drive. If, however, we are stopped for speeding ourselves we may protest that this is not our 'normal' pattern of behaviour but that there are exceptional circumstances that explain this one transgression.

Another explanation of the actor-observer bias relates to the fact that each will have a different perspective on the behaviour in question. If we are paying close attention to the old man who falls from his bike this image will dominate our visual field and, as a result we may presume that he alone is responsible for his fate. By comparison if it is ourselves in the situation we will be looking around at the environment and immediately notice the large pothole that accounted for our fall from grace.

The actor-observer bias does not necessarily occur in every situation. For example, if we feel empathy towards the other person we may be more likely to use the same attribution as the person whom we are observing. However, as we will see later, in circumstances in which we already feel prejudiced against the sort of person whom we witness suffering some misfortune, we may be even more likely to offer a dispositional explanation. By contrast, if we have a high opinion of ourselves and of our abilities we may be even less inclined to admit any responsibility for bad things that happen to us. If the car in front of us stalls at the traffic lights, we will presume that the driver is incompetent, especially if the driver is a member of a different sex or race. Of course if *we* stall the car at the lights we will be able to come up with a number of explanations that avoid the need to think of ourselves as an incompetent driver.

One other important phenomenon that has been found by researchers is known as the *self-serving attributional* bias. This refers to the fact that we often like to take credit for things that go well and deny responsibility for things that go badly. Thus if people are asked to explain their success on an important examination they may claim proudly that it was down to their ability and hard work. On the other hand if people are asked to account for their failure, they may look for an explanation that shifts the responsibility elsewhere – in this case perhaps towards an external source in the form of an unfair examiner or poor teacher.

Making attributions in this way allows people to retain a positive view of themselves whilst still acknowledging that they have failed in some way. In other words people might maintain a positive self-image by not accepting responsibility directly for something bad that happened. In some cases people may be prepared to admit some degree of responsibility so long as this does not challenge their largely positive view of themselves. For example the person may decide that they failed the examination because they were not able to put enough time and effort into the preparation. This explanation will lead the person to believe that if only they do a little more work next time they will surely be able to pass.

We can thus see that whilst making attributions is an important part of everyday life, people are not always fair, objective, or accurate in the attributions that they make. As we will see in the next section, once prejudice and stereotyping are added to the equation, there is a great deal of scope for mistaken attributions. If police officers are aware of the way that people typically make attributions, and of the systematic errors that can creep in, they may be less likely to make inappropriate judgements about the actions of others. Not everyone who behaves badly is doing so simply because they are a bad person. And not everyone who becomes a victim should be made to feel responsible for their own victimisation. Most psychologists would today go beyond a simple consideration of dispositional factors when trying to explain people's behaviour. If police officers can do the same, they may gain a much better insight into the many factors that, collectively, might explain why a criminal behaved the way that they did on a particular occasion. Initiatives such as situational crime prevention (Hough *et al*, 1980) provide one example of this wider focus. Systematic crime analysis and offender profiling (see chapter 9) can also help to prevent police officers from making simplistic and inappropriate attributions about the behaviour of others.

Prejudice and stereotyping

We have already seen in this and the previous chapter that a great deal of person perception relies upon us placing those that we meet into categories. Doing this allows us to have available some additional information about the sort of person with whom we are interacting. Placing people into categories almost inevitably leads us to use stereotypes about the person. To stereotype is, according to Aronson (1999: 307), to:

Assign identical characteristics to any person in a group regardless of the actual variation among members of that group.

Thus whilst stereotyping allows us to simplify our social world, it is also potentially dangerous in that it blinds us to individual differences between members of the stereotyped group. If your stereotype leads you to believe that women are bad drivers or that Afro-Caribbeans smoke marijuana you will tend to presume that *every* woman you meet will be a bad driver or that *every* Afro-Caribbean you come across will be a drug user. Such views may be stereotypical but they also tend to reflect prejudice against members of other groups. Prejudice has been defined in a number of different ways, although Aronson (1999: 305) offers a succinct definition in suggesting that it is:

A hostile or negative attitude toward a distinguishable group based on generalisations derived from faulty or incomplete information.

In general the word prejudice is used to refer to negative *attitudes* whilst discrimination relates to negative *behaviour*. One immediate problem is that whilst we can legislate against discrimination (i.e. negative behaviour) we may be able to do little to affect people's negative attitudes. A police officer who harbours a great deal of racial prejudice may go unchallenged so long as their views are not overheard by senior officers and their actions on the streets do not lead to a sustainable charge of harassment.

There would appear to be a direct link between prejudice and stereotyping, though the link may work in both directions. For example, if you are prejudiced against members of a certain ethnic group the chances are that your prejudice will lead you to stereotype all members of the group. Using expressions such as 'They're all the same, that lot' reinforces such a link. But the relationship can also be in the opposite direction. If you already hold stereotypes about members of a certain group the chances are that you will act in a prejudiced way towards members of that group.

Prejudice and policing

Prejudice and discrimination have become important topics both within psychology and in the world in general. Recognition of the existence of racism, sexism, ageism etc. has persuaded many governments to act by introducing legislation to try to prevent such blatant forms of discrimination. However, when accusations of prejudice and discrimination are levelled at law enforcement personnel, there is, understandably, cause for concern. There have been a number of high profile incidents in recent years in which white police officers have been accused of acting in racist ways. There are also a number of well-documented cases in which sexism within the police service has been demonstrated (Brown, 2000a). Police forces have been aware of the problems that prejudice can cause in areas such as law enforcement, yet have often been unable to tackle the problem effectively.

The recent admission by a number of senior British police officers that their organisations do suffer from 'institutional racism' came as something of a surprise. Since the publication of the Scarman report (1981) British police forces have consistently claimed that they have made progress in reducing the problem of racism within the service. However, when senior officers are prepared to admit that this is not the case, this raises a number of issues. The recent publication of the MacPherson report (1999), which suggested that prejudice was widespread within the Metropolitan Police, has prompted many forces to address issues of racism in a more systematic way.

In the USA, incidents such as the televised beating of Rodney King by white police officers sent out shock waves and aroused a chorus of concern about this type of apparently racist attack. Following the broadcast of such disturbing images many other people came forward with stories of similar assaults. There are also some disturbing practices that appear to perpetuate prejudiced views of ethnic minorities. For example, in some US police forces it is common practice to record black on black shootings as 'NHI'. This abbreviation is of the expression 'No Humans Involved' which is perhaps one of the worst examples of prejudice and stereotyping.

One might have thought that, as society has tried to legislate against prejudice and discrimination in recent years, practices of this kind would have long since been eradicated. However, it would appear that at least in the case of some police organisations, this has simply not happened. There are a number of reasons why this might be the case. First is the influence of the so-called 'canteen culture' that operates within many police organisations (Ainsworth, 1995: 69). This notion refers to the tendency for police officers to have a way of viewing the world that is determined by the dominant sub-culture within their organisation. The expression 'canteen culture' refers to the typical banter to be heard when officers are together in the canteen (and away from the attentions of senior officers).

When a new recruit is beginning to learn the ropes they will tend to be influenced by what appear to be the dominant attitudes and beliefs of long-serving officers around them. Policing is a complex and difficult task at the best of times and it is understandable that the new recruit will look to others in an attempt to make the job more straightforward. Dividing the world up into different 'types' offers some hope for the recruit trying to simplify a complex world. However, as we have seen in this chapter, such division is likely to lead to prejudice and stereotyping.

It should be pointed out that these tendencies are not peculiar to the police service but may be 'typical' human traits. Most new recruits to any organisation will look to those around them to help in deciding how the job should be done. Psychologists such as Leon Festinger established many years ago that, when faced with uncertainty, individuals will look to others to help define their social reality (Festinger, 1954). Festinger's research led him to develop his *social comparison theory* which suggests that people do indeed look to others when they are unsure of how they should feel or act. Other early social psychological research (e.g. Asch, 1951) also demonstrated that groups can exert a powerful influence over individuals and persuade them that conformity to the group norm is to be expected. Police work can be a dangerous occupation and contains a number of uncertainties and contradictions. One way in which these challenges can be addressed is by a strong sense of group loyalty and solidarity. These conditions may however have the effect of encouraging an 'us and them' mentality in which most of those outside the organisation are perceived negatively.

Writing in 1987 the current author and a colleague stated somewhat provocatively that:

> If you were a racist when you started this book, you will almost certainly still be a racist when, or rather if, you finish it.
>
> (Ainsworth and Pease, 1987: 103)

This statement was intended not to suggest that people never change, but rather that change is difficult, especially if one is surrounded by others who appear not to wish to change. Whilst senior police officers may try hard to reduce prejudice within their organisations, if the dominant sub-culture refuses to change, little progress will be made. The findings that have emerged from many years of research into topics such as prejudice allow us a much clearer understanding of the concepts and of the reasons for their existence. Some have argued that prejudice should be seen not as some deviant human trait that should be eradicated but rather as a 'normal' aspect of human behaviour. Cochrane (1991: 127) states that:

> What is important about the findings that prejudice is very common is that any explanation for it must recognise that it is a statistically 'normal' psychological phenomena and not an aberration limited to a minority of unstable or disturbed people.

This viewpoint is certainly interesting. It suggests that police forces that vow to remove prejudice from their ranks completely will have an uphill struggle. If police officers are expected to be representative of the communities from which they are drawn then they might be expected to be just as prejudiced as other members of the community.

Cochrane's viewpoint is based upon some of the psychological research that we have considered already, but also draws upon research on *ethnocentrism* and *social identity theory*. We will consider these now.

Ethnocentrism and social identity theory

Ethnocentrism refers to the human tendency to see ourselves and the groups to which we belong as the central focus of our world. Each group (be this racial, occupational or whatever) tends to nourish pride in itself and presumes itself to be superior to other alternative groups. Groups thus emphasise the aspects that make their group distinctive and in doing so tend to encourage their members to feel good about their group and 'bad' about the alternative group(s). Thus football supporters of one team will be encouraged to feel good about being a member of their own group and grateful that they are not members of the alternate (and presumably inferior) group. Being told that Club X has 'the best supporters in the world' makes each supporter of Club X feel good about themselves and glad that they are not members of the supporters' club of Team Y.

If ethnocentrism served merely to foster pride in oneself and one's group then it would pose few problems. However, the flip side of feeling good about one's own 'in-group' is feeling negatively towards members of the other 'out-group'. Being made to feel good about being a young white male can serve to make one feel bad about others who are not young, white or male. Police forces that foster a great deal of self pride and belief may, however unintentionally, encourage 'insiders' to think less well of 'outsiders' (Ainsworth, 1995: 65). Ethnocentrism will of course tend to have an effect upon the attributions that we make about others' behaviour – 'bad' deeds perpetrated by members of our own group will tend to be seen less negatively than the same actions committed by members of the other group. The actions of a police officer who hits a prisoner may receive little negative comment from colleagues, yet a prisoner who hits a police officer may be judged much more harshly.

Ethnocentrism is a very common human trait that appears to have its roots in humans' need to have some degree of self-esteem and a positive self-image. As noted above, emphasising the positive aspects of one's own group and the negative aspects of others serves to make people feel generally good about themselves. Brown (1986) suggests that, whilst ethnocentrism is often associated with hostility and even violence towards members of other groups, this is not inevitable. Brown argues that the additional factor of comparability comes into play here. According to Brown, hostility is more likely when groups perceive themselves to be comparable to others, but that the 'others' have an unfair or unjust disadvantage. Thus when, in 2001, some long term residents of a run-down area of Glasgow perceived that asylum seekers were getting a better deal than themselves, there was a great deal of hostility.

Social identity theory was developed by Henry Tajfel (Tajfel, 1971). The theory follows on from the work on ethnocentrism in suggesting that when people join a group, any group, they immediately and auto-matically think of that group as better than the alternative. People do this in order to enhance their self-esteem, but also in order to establish their social identity. If we are asked to describe ourselves to someone who has never met us before, we may well describe our membership of certain groups. In doing this we are providing examples of our social identities. A man who describes himself as 'a senior police officer', 'a Christian' and 'a member of the Freemasons' has provided three examples of group membership and thus social identity.

Ethnocentrism, stereotyping, and prejudice appear to be inextricably linked (Brown, 1986). In addition we must bear in mind that the attributions that we make about others' behaviour will be affected by all three human tendencies (Duncan, 1976). As such our desire to construct a social reality should perhaps be seen not as an objective attempt to understand the world around us but more as a subjective construction based upon our own needs and desires. Police trainers and managers who recognise that this is the case may be able to go some way towards reducing the amount of prejudice shown by their officers

Summary

In this chapter we have considered the attributions that people make about others' behaviour. We have seen that in many cases these attributions are neither objective nor accurate. A number of systematic biases in the attribution process have been identified and the consequences of each spelled out. We have also seen that prejudice is not necessarily an undesirable human trait that should be eradicated at all cost, but rather a 'normal' human tendency. Explanations for the occurrence of prejudice have been sought in the research on stereotyping, ethnocentrism, and social identity.

Prejudice may be a 'normal' human trait, but this does necessarily mean that we should simply wring our hands and give up hope of ever being able to tackle the problems that prejudice within an organisation such as the police service can cause. Stereotyping may also be a very common human tendency for it has a utilitarian value in helping to simplify a complex human world. However, this does not mean that the consequences of the use of undesirable stereotypes should go unchallenged. For this reason the current author would argue that police training programmes should incorporate some teaching based upon the psychological research on prejudice and stereotyping. But so long as the majority of police officers hold stereotypical and perhaps prejudiced views of psychology and psychologists, this may not happen immediately.

Much of this chapter has been taken up with a discussion of how police officers interact with members of the public, be they witnesses, victims or suspects. But of course prejudice may also reveal itself in the way in which officers interact with their colleagues. A sexist, racist, male police officer will tend to behave in a prejudiced way when working with a female colleague or with one from an ethnic minority. As long as the majority of Western police forces remain dominated by white males, the way in which minorities within the service are treated may remain a potential source of unrest.

Further reading

Aronson, E. (1999) *The Social Animal*. New York: Worth; Chapter 7.

Brown, J. (2000) *Gender & Policing: Comparative Perspectives*. Basingstoke: MacMillan.

Brown, R. (1986) *Social Psychology* (2nd ed). New York: Free Press; Chapters 15 and 16.

Chapter 3

Recruitment, selection and training

In order for any law enforcement organisation to function efficiently and effectively it is essential that it employs those individuals who are best suited to the complex task of policing. Police organisations need to ensure that they employ the sort of individual who possesses those qualities that are deemed to be essential to the job. They must, however, avoid recruiting any individual who possesses qualities that are deemed to be unacceptable to the police organisation.

Psychology has made great advances in recent years in the testing of individuals in order to ascertain their personality, IQ, values etc. The number and type of psychometric tests available has proliferated substantially as employers have demanded more help in making decisions about applicants to their organisations. It would thus seem appropriate that psychology should be used to help police forces ensure that they recruit the most appropriate people for the job. However, this is not always as straightforward as one might presume. In this chapter we will look at some of the main issues around the use of testing and also consider what psychology may have to offer in the training of police officers.

Should psychological testing be used at all?

One of the first issues that should be addressed in relation to the testing of police recruits is whether it should be used at all. Historically, many police forces have been reluctant to use psychometric tests to aid their selection procedures. For a number of years there was a belief by many within police organisations that they already knew what sort of person they needed to join their ranks. Furthermore, it was generally felt that it was relatively easy to spot the 'right' sort of person during the sifting of application forms and while conducting interviews with applicants. However, more recently many police forces have started to use psychometric tests as an aid to selection. In two recent small-scale surveys in the US it was reported that approximately one third of police psychologists' time is spent on selection and screening activities (Bergen *et al*, 1992; Bartol, 1996).

In addition to the obvious point of 'recruiting the right sort of person' there are other reasons why police organisations might consider using psychometric tests. Firstly police forces may need to protect themselves from accusations of bias in their selection procedures. Thus if an organisation rejects a high proportion of ethnic minority or female applicants, they will need to be able to demonstrate that their procedures have nevertheless been 'fair'. This is a particular issue for law enforcement agencies in the USA where litigation may follow if organisations are unable to demonstrate the fairness of their selection procedures (Super, 1999). Hibler and Kurke (1995: 71) make the point that law enforcement agencies may be liable if they discriminate unlawfully against certain applicants, but may also be liable if they hire someone who then harms a member of the public whilst performing their duties.

Another reason that psychological screening is important concerns the cost of training. Estimates of these costs vary according to the organisation, but an officer who is judged to be unsuitable after many months of training will represent a considerable drain on resources. Fitzsimmons (1986) suggested that in the US, each employment 'error' (i.e. hiring an unsuitable officer) could cost the city almost $500,000. Similarly an officer who commits an act that results in litigation against the organisation (e.g. the shooting of an unarmed suspect) will be a significant 'cost' in terms of both money and reputation.

Many police forces will have considered using psychometric tests to aid in their selection processes. The use of such tests goes back over 80 years, when rudimentary intelligence tests were used to identify suitable applicants for the police service (Terman and Otis, 1917). One should not, however, presume that the introduction of testing is solely because enlightened police organisations have seen the value of psychology. Super (1999: 409) suggests that another important reason, at least in the USA, is that by using psychological services, police chiefs can increase indemnity for themselves and their agency.

How can psychological testing help?

Let us consider for a moment what may happen if no psychological tests are used. It was noted above that some police officers may hold on to the view that they can spot a good recruit easily. The problem with such a belief is that it appears to rely a great deal on 'instinct' or 'gut feeling'. Those involved in the selection procedure may claim that, after years in the job, they can tell who will and who will not make 'a good copper'. Yet if they were to be questioned as to how they reached such a decision they may well find it difficult to identify the exact criteria upon which these important decisions might be based.

As noted above, police forces that rely on the 'instincts' of those involved in the recruitment process may stand accused of prejudice and bias if they are unable to list some objective criteria by which applicants are judged. It would be all too easy for a white, male, middle class recruitment officer to judge others by reference to his own values and beliefs. As such the black, female, working class applicant may not even get through the first sifting of applications. We saw in the previous chapter how person perception relies to a great extent on stereotyping. If those involved in the recruitment process have stereotypical (and possibly incorrect) views about who will and who will not make good police officers, it is possible that many applicants who might otherwise be recruited and have a positive influence on the organisation will fall at the first hurdle. Police forces are generally known for their conservatism and tradition. As a result they may be reluctant to recruit those who appear to challenge the conservative norms that have been established over time. In any large bureaucratic organisation, change tends to be evolutionary rather than revolutionary.

Psychometric testing represents an attempt to bring more objectivity into the decision making progress. Rather than relying upon gut feelings and instincts it offers standardised testing procedures by which people can be evaluated. For example, if it is felt that police officers need to have a certain level of intelligence, it would be a fairly straightforward matter to administer an appropriate IQ test to all applicants. Those who reach the agreed level might thus be included in the next round of the selection process whilst those who do not would be rejected outright. This type of psychometric testing can be useful in that it allows police forces to 'screen out' at an early stage those who are considered unsuitable. Provided the police organisation can identify a list of criteria that applicants must fulfil, it is a fairly straightforward matter to devise tests that will identify those who do and those who do not meet these criteria. The problem, however, is that it is not always obvious which criteria should be included within the testing procedures. Furthermore, as we will see later in this chapter, screening out unsuitable applicants may be only half the battle – identifying those who would make the best police officers might represent a different problem.

What qualities should psychological tests be looking for?

When we start to think about the criteria that should be included in any initial screening we begin to see some of the problems. Whilst some criteria (e.g. a certain level of IQ) are fairly obvious, others are not. Presumably we would want our initial screening to identify people who are honest and trustworthy but beyond that it becomes a little more difficult. Should we for example try to identify and rule out those who appear to be prejudiced against ethnic minorities? Should we consider only those who have good social skills and can relate well to others? Should we exclude all those who have any form of criminal record no matter how trivial?

In making such decisions we may wish to consider some of the research on attribution (see Chapter 2). Taking the example of the prejudiced applicant, we might decide that their prejudice is a deep seated aspect of their personality that is unlikely ever to change. As a result we would probably exclude this applicant from further consideration. On the other hand we may decide that their prejudice is something that has come about as a result of some recent external influence and may thus be easily modified through appropriate training and education. Given the claim by Cochrane (1991) that prejudice is a 'normal' tendency for humans we may even begin to question whether we should try to screen out those who show what may be normal or average levels of prejudice (see Chapter 2).

Many job advertisements will provide a list of essential qualities that all applicants must possess, along with a list of other desirable qualities. The problem in terms of police applicants is that it is surprisingly difficult to construct a list upon which all police employers would agree. In the UK the Home Office lays down a number of 'minimum requirements' that applicants should possess, but beyond this each force can to some extent set their own criteria. One might thus find that an applicant who is rejected as unsuitable by one organisation may be accepted by its neighbour.

At the time of writing, the Home Office is attempting to introduce national recruitment standards for police officers in the UK. The Advisory Group on National Recruitment Standards (AGNRS) has made a number of recommendations including:

- No formal educational qualifications should be required but there continues to be a need for some kind of written ability test.

- The Police Initial Recruitment Test (PIRT) should be reviewed to ensure that it is job-related, non-discriminatory and still valid.

- The Home Office should issue guidelines on dyslexic candidates.

- There should be no upper age limit for entry (although the normal retirement age is 55, and applicants will need to satisfy all the criteria for entry including the medical and physical requirements).

- There should be consistency in policy with regard to a range of diverse criteria including: criminal convictions, tattoos, driving and swimming skills, checking for solvency, obtaining references, security checks and repeat applications.

These proposals would clearly introduce some consistency in recruitment, although consistency does not necessarily equate with effectiveness. Few of the criteria outlined above appear to guarantee that the police service would recruit the most able candidates or those most suited to the complex task of policing. For example, scores on the PIRT do not necessarily correlate with performance at police training school (Addison, 2000). The other problem with establishing national guidelines is that they take little account of the differences involved in policing different parts of the country. There is often a world of difference between policing inner city areas and policing rural and scattered communities.

What qualities should the police look for in recruits?

Returning to the issue of the qualities that recruits should possess, it can prove difficult to identify what these should be. Blau (1994: 72) suggests that in the US, police managers frequently use the following criteria as defining the 'good cop':

- Bravery or courage
- Decisiveness
- Consistency and reliability
- Resistance to stress
- Cooperativeness
- Traditional values
- Respect for authority.

It is interesting to note that amongst these qualities, the last three seem to have more to do with recruits 'fitting in' with the organisation than carrying out the role of policing effectively. This appears to reinforce the view expressed earlier of an organisation that is traditional and conservative and that does not welcome change readily.

If one looks at recruiting advertisements for the police service, one may come away somewhat confused. One survey that looked at advertisements in the UK found that recurring themes were *common sense*, an *ability to work with and relate to people*, and *a sense of humour* (Ainsworth, 1996). This same study also asked a small group of serving police officers for their views. The top four qualities listed were: *sense of humour, communication skills, adaptability*, and *common sense*. The problem with a number of these 'qualities' is that they are somewhat difficult to measure using psychometric tests. And even for those qualities for which good tests already exist, it may not be easy to reach a consensus on the levels at which people must perform in order to be deemed suitable. If we take the example of *sense of humour*, we can see the problem. Not only is this all but impossible to measure accurately, even if we could do so we may run into difficulties. Some people might appear to have a lot of this quality, yet it may also be noted that theirs is a 'strange' sense of humour. Indicators such as 'common sense' may be equally if not more difficult to measure objectively. As Blau (1994: 72) notes, whilst some of the qualities that make a good police officer may be described, less tangible measures such as being 'street smart', defy definition and measurement.

There is thus a danger that psychometric tests will be used to measure those qualities that are easily measured yet are not the most important. Conversely some qualities that might be seen as more important will go untested. This is a problem similar to that encountered when devising performance indicators. Whilst some aspects of performance are easily measured (e.g. how long it takes for the phone to be answered) others that may be more important for customer satisfaction (e.g. how helpful the person who answered the phone actually was) may go unmeasured.

Hibler and Kurke (1995: 60) suggest that there are a number of criteria that make up what they term 'psychological suitability'. They say:

> The first priority is for people with psychological integrity, the second is for those people to effectively deal with a wide range of demands that are made on them in the course of serving the public.

These authors go on to suggest that officers should have emotional stability but also have the necessary interpersonal skills to deal with a range of emotional states. Police officers need to be able to deal effectively with both distressed individuals and those expressing a great deal of anger and hostility. The skills required for the former (e.g. empathy) may be negatively correlated with those required for the latter. It is this diversity of demands and skills required that can make selection difficult and is the reason why 'adaptability' is seen as a desirable quality.

Hibler and Kurke use the term 'psychological integrity' but do not make it clear what is meant by this term. Absence of pathology and emotional stability would appear to be included within the term. There is, however, a need to measure integrity itself – a police officer who becomes unreliable or even corrupt will cost the organisation a great deal in terms of respect and reputation. Unfortunately, the accurate testing of honesty and integrity has proved to be somewhat difficult. Many of the tests used appear to produce a high number of 'false positives' (i.e. people who are honest and have integrity are accused of not being so). Furthermore, Blau (1994: 72) notes that, although there are more than 40 different integrity tests available, hardly any studies of these tests have been published in academic journals.

As we have seen, policing is a varied occupation needing perhaps a large number of diverse skills. Furthermore, all police organisations will contain a number of different departments within which officers are required to do very different kinds of work. In the UK and in many other countries, all those who become specialists or senior officers will have risen through the ranks, having joined as humble young constables. Given this fact it may be difficult to identify a set of core skills or qualities that every applicant, regardless of their ultimate position within the organisation, must possess. The skills needed to be a successful dog handler, criminal intelligence analyst or Chief Constable must surely have little in common, yet each of these people will have had to fit the basic criteria laid down for all recruits.

In deciding what qualities should be sought in the new recruit it is perhaps best to consider three different criteria:

1. What qualities does the applicant already possess that would appear to make them suitable for the job of policing?

2. What qualities does the person currently lack and can any of these be rectified through education or appropriate training?

3. What qualities does the person possess that would deem them unsuitable for police work at present?

What these three questions force us to do is to consider whether there are core skills or qualities that are essential to the job, or whether the majority of attributes can be taught through training. They also force us to consider whether some attributes that would bar certain individuals from being considered for police work could be removed through appropriate training. Someone who suffers from a severe personality disorder may be unsuitable no matter what training or education was offered. On the other hand, an applicant who appears to have inappropriate attitudes and perceptions may be more likely to respond to training and may ultimately become a good police officer.

What problems might testing not be able to address?

Questions such as those above can become important if a police service decides that it needs to recruit officers from non-traditional sources or groups. For example it has been recognised for some time that within most British police forces, women and ethnic minorities are under-represented. In the case of ethnic minorities this has been a problem for two main reasons. Firstly, if the number of officers from ethnic minority backgrounds is very small, racist attitudes and stereotyping amongst white officers are likely to go unchallenged. Secondly, ethnic minority communities may feel that their needs are not met when their local police service has hardly any officers drawn from their own communities. These problems have been recognised for some time, although recent attempts to recruit more officers from ethnic minority communities in Britain have not met with a great deal of success. There is something of a 'chicken and egg' situation that can develop here. If a police force is perceived to be racist and has very few black officers, black people may be unlikely to consider applying. However, so long as the ratio of black to white officers remains low, the attitudes of the dominant group may go unchallenged and unchanged. Even if black officers can be recruited they are unlikely to stay in the job if they experience feelings of hostility or discrimination.

One interesting piece of research that illustrates the problem of testing was that carried out by Shusman and Inwald (1991). This study used a combination of the IPI (Inwald Personality Inventory) and the MMPI (Minnesota Multiphasic Personality Inventory) to assess 246 male correctional officers in the USA. They found that a discriminant function analysis of the two sets of results allowed them to differentiate between officers who appeared to be doing well in their careers and those who were performing less well up to three and a half years after joining the organisation. However, the criteria that were used to evaluate each officer's performance were the number of absences, the number of times the officer was late for duty, and the number of disciplinary interviews each officer had had. Clearly an officer who is persistently late, takes time off, and breaches disciplinary codes is not performing well, yet such measures can say little about how good the officer is at the actual job of policing. A recruit may rarely be late or absent, and may never be brought up on a disciplinary charge but may simply not be a 'good' police officer in terms of his/her relationship with the public, ability to detect crime etc.

Are the dimensions that are tested stable?

Another interesting point with regard to personality concerns the stability of personality dimensions. Some believe that personality attributes are 'fixed' whilst others believe that personality changes as a result of an individual's interactions and experiences with the world. Blau (1994) suggests that when police patrol officers are studied after only two years in the job there are significant personality, attitude and adjustment changes. He notes that officers:

> Showed more somatic symptoms, more anxiety, more alcohol-use vulnerability, and other traits that would have been considered significantly negative indicators at the time of recruitment.
>
> (Blau, 1994: 71)

Similarly Dunnette and Motowidlo (1976) found that the type of personality traits that are measured during recruitment selection often have little predictive value, because of the powerful influence of an officer's experiences in the job. This suggestion is supported by Lefkowitz (1977), who suggests that it is extremely difficult to predict future police performance because each year's experience in the job exposes officers to powerful influences that can shape their ideas, attitudes and behaviour. We will return to this notion in Chapter 8.

Gowan and Gatewood (1995) suggest that required qualities can be broken down into three main categories, i.e. *knowledge, skills* and *attributes*. Whilst some of these are relatively easily measured, others prove more difficult to evaluate. Furthermore, as we have noted above, there may be little agreement as to *which* knowledge, skills and attributes should be measured. In terms of qualities that may be lacking, Hibler and Kurke (1995: 80) make a distinction between *knowledge inadequacy* and *skill inadequacy*. They make the point that knowledge inadequacy is more easily addressed than skill inadequacy especially if the 'skill' in question is one that is a basic personality component rather than a 'skill' that can be learned and practised until a good level of competence is achieved.

How might tests be validated and evaluated?

Whatever tests are used, they will need to be valid and appropriate. Those working in the area talk of 'criterion referenced validation'. This terms refers to the fact that validation must relate to specific criteria. In other words we need to know whether scores on the psychological test correlate with some measure of job performance – if so then the test has high validity.

One way in which we may wish to carry out research is to subject a large number of serving police officers to a battery of tests and then see which of these tests allow us to differentiate between good and bad officers. We could then use the tests that were found to be the most useful on all those who apply to join the force. Those who match the profiles typically found in successful serving officers could then be selected. There is however a problem with this approach. What is actually being tested here is *concurrent* validity. What we should be using is some test that has *predictive* validity, i.e. something that allows us to identify which applicants are likely to become successful once they have undergone training and socialisation into the police role. As has been noted elsewhere:

> Test items that distinguish good and bad police officers *now* may be different from those that distinguish between people *who are likely to* **become** good police officers – i.e. those that can change and adapt most easily.

> (Ainsworth, 1996: 581)

Indeed, as was noted earlier, many of the skills and qualities that go to make a 'good' police officer may be those that have been produced during training, rather than those that the person has always possessed.

Job analysis and the combination of measures

One problem is that, whilst most people (especially those within the police organisation) will feel that they already 'know' what the job of policing involves, there have been relatively few comprehensive job analyses carried out. Until such time as we can establish exactly what tasks we expect police officers to be able to carry out effectively, it is difficult to start to be able to specify the skills and qualities that are required to do the job.

There have been some recent moves to try to establish both core and specific 'competencies' that might be involved in the task of policing. These have sought to establish a range of core behavioural competencies that are generic to all police employees. However, in addition, a database of job-specific skills and knowledge, along with a database of activities and tasks that make up the different jobs, needs to be established. Such systematic attempts to identify exactly what is needed for the many different roles that policing involves is perhaps an important first step.

One recent article has reviewed some 85 years of development in selection methods (Schmidt and Hunter, 1998). In this meta-analysis, Schmidt and Hunter suggest that certain types of tests, and certain combinations of testing procedures can have good predictive value in terms of future job performance. They note that, in general, factors such as an applicant's education and interests have quite low predictive validity and that graphology (i.e. handwriting analysis) has virtually none. By contrast, a General Mental Ability or GMA test (i.e. one that assesses a candidate's general mental abilities) or a work-sample method appear to have quite high predictive value.

Schmidt and Hunter conclude, however, that the best results can be obtained by a combination of a GMA and an integrity test, or by the combination of a GMA and a structured interview. The authors note that, despite recent developments in the field, many commercial employers are not using optimal selection methods and, as a result, may be losing millions of dollars in reduced production. Although police organisations may have different priorities, the point about sub-optimal performance and efficiency is still highly relevant.

Training and the acceptance of psychology

We have seen in this chapter that there are a number of important issues that affect selection and that psychology may be of some value in this process. However, it appears also to be true that psychology has something to offer in the training of police officers. It was noted earlier that selection may not necessarily be about selecting people with the 'right' qualities but rather be about selecting those who can change and adapt, and will benefit most from appropriate training. Psychometric tests can help to identify those who have the qualities that are deemed to be essential for the job of policing. However, as was noted earlier, recruits who lack certain skills might receive training that can fill or correct any skills deficit. Training might also be used to challenge inappropriate attitudes (e.g. those that are racist or sexist). Whilst no amount of training can turn a fundamentally unsuitable applicant into a competent officer, training can certainly give those with the appropriate potential, the skills and attributes that may be required.

It seems clear that the issues of selection and training are inextricably linked. For example we may decide that the police service would benefit if it accepts only those recruits who are above average in intelligence and have first degrees (Foster, 1998). However, if the initial training course that all new recruits are required to attend is not sufficiently geared to the needs and qualities of graduates, then there will inevitably be problems (Addison, 2000).

In Chapter 2 we suggested that knowledge of the psychological research on prejudice, attribution and stereotyping could be of some value in challenging prejudiced views. We also made the point in Chapter 1 that a knowledge of impression formation and non-verbal communication could be of considerable value to police officers. However, very few training courses currently include a significant amount of input on these topics. In future chapters (especially Chapters 6, 7 and 9) we will see other examples of how the results of psychological research can be applied productively to the police environment, providing they are taught appropriately.

In a number of branches of industry, 'multi-tasking' is becoming an important concept. Police trainers would probably want to point out that police officers have been multi-tasking for years, so diverse is the range of duties that the average police officer will be called upon to perform. Although officers' initial training will equip them to deal with some everyday situations, a great deal more training will be needed to turn the officer into an expert in any particular field of specialisation. Training will also be needed to keep officers up to date with changes in procedure and the law.

Who should conduct training?

In many cases, training will be carried out by those from within the organisation who are able to impart their legal and procedural knowledge to others. There remains a problem, however, with regard to the acceptance of knowledge imparted from those outside the organisation. Policing has often been described as a 'closed' culture in which 'outsiders' are treated with suspicion if not outright hostility (Ainsworth, 1995: Chapter 4). It is for this reason that relatively few psychologists will be involved in the day-to-day training of police officers. Attempts to introduce even basic psychology into the training of police officers has often met with some resistance (Bull and Horncastle, 1988). Even those police psychologists employed on a full-time basis tend to have comparatively little to do with the majority of training. There are of course some exceptions to this – as we will see in Chapter 10, psychologists can have some influence in areas such as hostage taking and negotiation. These instances are however the exception rather than the rule.

Even if it is accepted that knowledge of some relevant aspects of psychology would benefit all recruits, the delivery of such knowledge may pose further problems. We noted earlier that the police service tends to be quite insular and is reluctant to bring in outsiders on a large-scale basis. What typically happens is that a small number of people within the organisation receive specialist training, and these individuals then become trainers themselves. The problem when one applies this to an area such as psychology is perhaps obvious. Those allowed to call themselves 'psychologists' will have undergone between three and six years of training and will have followed a course of study largely prescribed by the governing body of psychology in their own country. Such regulation means that those who impart knowledge accumulated by the discipline of psychology have a good grounding in the subject and can draw upon a wide range of material. This contrasts sharply with the police trainer who may have attended a comparatively short training course and is then presumed to be sufficiently well versed in the subject to be able to teach it to a large number of others. Although a number of serving police officers will have degrees in psychology, it is rare that such officers will be engaged in the sorts of duties that allow them to apply their knowledge in the most productive way.

Even if the police organisation accepts that some aspect of psychology is highly relevant and should be brought to the attention of all police officers, there is no guarantee that this will be a successful exercise. We will see in Chapter 6 that attempts to introduce such apparently valuable tools as the cognitive interview technique have not had the success that was anticipated. Even when a change in something as fundamental as the interviewing of suspects, victims and witnesses is attempted, there is no guarantee that a positive change in practice will ensue (Clarke and Milne, 2001).

We can thus see that while there are clear benefits that might result from a greater involvement of psychologists and psychology in police training, acceptance by those within the organisation may be slow. At present there are perhaps two types of psychologists whose work will be of relevance to policing. First would come police psychologists themselves who, one might presume, would have a very large impact on training and yet who typically do not. Second would come those psychologists whose research and knowledge would have tangible benefits to police officers if only their work was brought to the attention of officers, especially those undergoing training. It is unfortunate that at the present time the attitude of many within police organisations means that psychology will remain a 'fringe' subject whose value may not be appreciated fully.

'Training' today means much more than sitting in a classroom and being filled with knowledge. The introduction of role-plays, experiential learning, problem solving exercises and on-the-job training has had significant benefits. However, White and Honig (1995: 258) note that training has become an elaborate and diversified field but that:

> This diversity is a mixed blessing for the police psychologist. Although it offers unlimited possibilities in terms of how to train, who to train and what to train, it also creates a deal of complexity. Designing a training program that addresses the multilevel needs of an organisation such as law enforcement can be extremely challenging.

These authors suggest that there are a large number of ways in which psychology can be used in the training process. Some of these include wellness training, informational and skills training, and organisational training. However, as these and other writers have acknowledged, getting the police to see the potential benefits of such inputs may not be straightforward. We should also admit that psychologists not accustomed to working in the sort of environment that law enforcement occupies may have to be creative in the work that they employ. White and Honig (1995: 276) suggest that psychologists will need to use a combination of perseverance, flexibility and versatility if they are to succeed. They will also need to draw upon a wide range of material ranging from organisational, clinical, educational, social and forensic psychology.

Summary

In this chapter we have discussed a number of issues surrounding the application of psychology to the areas of selection and training. We saw in the early part of the chapter that while psychology has made enormous advances in the area of testing and selection, there are a number of problems associated with the use of such tests in police recruit selection. The introduction of comprehensive job analyses would be an important first step in helping psychologists to develop the most appropriate type of selection process. However, the extremely varied nature of police work means that it will be difficult to devise simple tests by which all applicants should be judged. It is, however, important that the area should continue to develop. The costs of employing the 'wrong' type of person can be substantial both in terms of financial costs and the cost to the organisation's reputation. There may also be difficulty in attracting people from ethnic minority communities (Stone and Tuffin, 2000).

We have also seen in this chapter that while psychologists could make valuable inputs into the training process, to date their influence has not been substantial. There remains a reluctance within many police organisations to accept the potential benefits of psychological research and knowledge. We also noted that whilst selection and training are often treated as separate entities, the two are inextricably linked. As (Hibler and Kurke, 1995: 90) note:

> The needs of communities served by the police in the 21st century are best understood in terms of a multifaceted personnel preparation capability in which selection, training, and caring for the force are well integrated and mutually complementary.

Further reading

Anderson, N. and Herriot, P. (eds.) (1997) *International Handbook of Selection and Assessment*. Chichester: Wiley.

Kurke, M. I. and Scrivner, E. M. (eds.) (1995) *Police Psychology into the 21st Century*. Hillsdale NJ: LEA.

Stone, R. and Tuffin, R. (2000) *Attitudes of People from Minority Ethnic Communities towards a Career in the Police Service*. Police Research Series, Paper 136. London: Home Office PRCU.

Chapter 4

Aggression and violence

Amongst the many duties that police officers will be called upon to perform, dealing with individuals who are behaving in violent or aggressive ways may be at the forefront of many people's image of the police. Dealing with violent youths who have been on a drinking binge, calming the irate man who seems intent on harming his partner, controlling a group of football hooligans, are all incidents with which we expect police officers to deal. Police officers may have their own views as to why people become violent and aggressive, and have their own ways of dealing with those who exhibit these tendencies.

Violence and aggression are often portrayed as representing threats to the civilised world and for this reason psychologists and other social scientists have studied the phenomenon extensively. As with so many aspects of human behaviour it is not possible to come up with one simple answer to the question of why people behave in these ways. However, the enormous amount of research that has been conducted allows us to have a much better understanding of the many factors that contribute to such behaviour. In this chapter we will examine a number of prominent theories of aggression and consider how these might aid our understanding both in terms of causation and response. We will also consider some of the factors that might contribute to police officers behaving in violent and aggressive ways.

Defining aggression and violence

One immediate problem that we encounter when we start to think about violence and aggression is one of definition. While we all 'know' what the terms mean, their exact definition can often prove difficult. A member of a gang who targets and then kills a member of a rival gang is clearly behaving in an aggressive and violent way. But would we also include in our definition the male company director who is said to be 'ruthless' and 'aggressive' in his dealings with others? Psychologists have generally carried out their research on aggression rather than violence *per se*. Even here though exact definitions prove difficult to agree upon. Geen (2001: 3) offers a useful working definition of the concept in suggesting that it is:

> The delivery of an aversive stimulus from one person to another, with intent to harm and with an expectation of causing such harm, when the other person is motivated to escape or avoid the stimulus.

Researchers have identified a number of different types of aggressive acts that may have different motivations. One of the main distinctions is that between *affective* and *instrumental* aggression. Affective aggression is generally associated with anger and in such cases the primary motive is the harming of the victim him/herself. By contrast instrumental aggression is not necessarily associated with emotions such as anger but occurs as a means to an end. The desperate addict who assaults the pharmacist in order to get supplies of a favoured drug may be using aggression in an instrumental way in order to achieve some other objective – in this case supplies of the drug. In many cases affective aggression comes about as a result of some form of provocation and the angry response is aimed primarily at harming the person who is the source of the provocation. In most cases the provocation leads to physiological arousal but the feeling is more complex than simply getting angry (Frijda, 1994). By contrast the infliction of harm in the form of instrumental aggression is not necessarily accompanied by any particular emotional state. Whilst the distinction between these two forms of aggression can be useful there are inevitably some instances in which the two overlap.

A similar distinction that has been made is between *reactive* and *proactive* aggression (Crick and Dodge, 1996). The first of these is similar to the notion of affective aggression discussed above in that it refers to aggressive behaviour that occurs in response to verbal or physical provocation and results in both angry actions and self-defence. By contrast proactive aggression, as its name implies, refers to aggression that occurs without any form of initial provocation and involves violence that is committed in order to gain some reward, be it monetary or psychological (e.g. intimidation or respect). The majority of psychological research has been concerned with affective rather than instrumental aggression. This is unfortunate especially for those involved in law enforcement as some of the aggression that will be encountered will be of the latter type.

We will see in this chapter that a large number of theories have emerged in response to the question of why people commit violent or aggressive acts. As in other areas of psychology, a distinction is often attempted between those factors that lie within the individual him/ herself and those that are related to the situational context in which the aggression occurs. In the former category would be genetic factors, and those pertaining to the background of the individual. In the latter would be the myriad situational factors that may have combined to produce an aggressive outburst. It would, however, be inappropriate to treat these two sets of variables completely separately as in many cases it is the interaction between the two that best explains an aggressive act.

We will start our examination of some theories of aggression with a discussion as to whether aggression is seen best as a naturally occurring human phenomenon or as a learned response.

Aggression as an innate drive

One of the first questions we may wish to ask is whether aggression should be seen as an innate factor in humans. Some commentators have pointed to the fact that throughout history, humans have invariably behaved aggressively and violently especially towards their fellow human beings. No animal species on earth comes close to humans in terms of the number of their own kind that they have killed. As Storr (1970: 11) notes: 'there is no parallel in nature to our savage treatment of each other'. One need think only of the numbers killed during any recent war to offer support for such a stance. Unlike feared animals such as sharks or tigers, humans rarely kill for food nor, in many cases, for self-protection. The American social psychologist Eliot Aronson comments on the fact that any human history will contain a list of many events in which millions of people have been killed. Such a realisation prompts him to ask 'What kind of species are we if the most important events in the brief history of humankind are situations in which people kill one another *en masse*?' (Aronson, 1999: 254). Given these facts it is perhaps understandable that some writers have suggested that aggression is a 'naturally' occurring human trait.

Such a view was expressed by one of the founding fathers of psychology, Sigmund Freud (1930). Freud believed that humans' aggressive tendencies came about as a result of an innate driving force that is present in all people. Freud postulated that there were in fact two driving forces within each human, i.e. *Eros*, that was an instinct towards life, and *Thanatos*, that was a death instinct and led to aggressive actions.

Rather than suggesting that people learn to become violent as they grow up, Freud believed that humans have this innate driving force within them from birth. Because of this viewpoint, Freud suggested that the best that society could hope for was to channel these aggressive instincts into socially acceptable forms of expression. If society did not provide such opportunities, the pressure within each individual would build up to a certain level at which point there would be an explosion of violence and aggression. Violent sports such as boxing provide an obvious example of how such a build-up might be avoided, although Freud even suggested that wars sanctioned by governments gave people the opportunity to release some of their in-built aggressive urges. Freud was not the first to hold this viewpoint, indeed Thomas Hobbes writing in the 17th century had also suggested that humans had a naturally aggressive nature (Hobbes, 1651).

Like many of Freud's views it is difficult to prove categorically whether he is right or wrong. It is difficult to imagine how one might test his hypothesis experimentally. Some of the research that has been carried out on other species of animals appears to offer somewhat contradictory findings. Whilst people such as Lorenz (1966) have argued that humans share an in-built fighting instinct with many other animal species, other researchers have suggested that many animals will only attack others if there is a need to do so (Scott, 1958).

There do appear to be some questions that might be raised in response to Freud's basic hypothesis. For example we may wish to point to the fact that most people do not behave violently and aggressively most of the time. Furthermore different societies and cultures appear to have different levels of violence and aggression within them or even different levels at different times in history. Members of some societies appear able to settle disputes without resorting to force, yet for others, violent confrontation is the norm. Similarly if aggression is an innate tendency why is it that in most societies males are considerably more violent than females? Even within the male population, some individuals appear to have a calmness that means that they never become involved in acts of aggression, while others live on the edge of confrontation almost constantly. Even if there is some value in Freud's views it is clearly far too simplistic an explanation for the majority of aggression.

Some appear to support Freud's viewpoint by suggesting that aggression is an innate driving force in the sense that it has some survival value. To put it bluntly, humans who are unable to defend themselves against physical threats are unlikely to live long enough to be able to procreate. In other words whilst aggressive tendencies may lead to the killing of large numbers of others, they may also ensure the survival of the species as a whole. For example, Lore and Schultz (1993) have suggested that aggression is a common feature in the lives of most animal species for the simple reason that it has some survival value.

A similar view has been expressed by Buss and Kenrick (1998), who offer some support for this sociobiological perspective on aggression. However, even writers such as these agree that most animals have also developed mechanisms that enable them to suppress such aggressive instincts when it is in their interests to do so. For example if we are threatened by an extremely large and aggressive-looking man carrying a gun, it may be in our interests to suppress our desire to behave aggressively towards this person. Thus it is suggested that, even in the most violent species, aggression remains an option rather than an automatic response as Freud had originally suggested. Most commentators would agree that while approaches such as those of the sociobiologists may shed some light on the biological underpinnings of aggression, they are in themselves insufficient to explain the myriad aggressive behaviours of which humans are capable.

Aggression as a response to external stimuli

Earlier in this chapter we suggested that in many cases aggression arises as a result of provocation. There are, however, other events or situations that might trigger the aggressive response. One of these is the experience of frustration. Such a suggestion was first made by Dollard and his colleagues more than 60 years ago when they developed the *frustration-aggression hypothesis* (Dollard *et al*, 1939). Dollard and his colleagues suggested quite simply that when a person experiences frustration of some kind, they will be inclined to react to such frustration by behaving aggressively. Furthermore Dollard suggested that, whenever a person is seen to be acting aggressively, their behaviour can be traced back to the experience of frustration.

Such a belief is somewhat sweeping, yet it does seem to have some intrinsic appeal. If we are experiencing frustration and are unable to attain some goal or other, we do sometimes become angry and perhaps aggressive, especially towards the source of the frustration. Thus if the car in front of us stalls and causes us to miss the traffic lights, we may shout abuse at the other driver or even threaten them with violence. However, even in this example, we may note that not all frustrated drivers would react in this way. We may also observe that there are a large number of precursors of aggression, only one of which is the experience of frustration.

It does now seem that the original frustration-aggression hypothesis was far too general and simplistic. However, this does not mean that it has no value. Some more recent research has supported the proposition that the experience of frustration can create an instigation to aggress. For example Novaco (1991) suggested that 'road rage' attacks could be related to motorists' experience of severe traffic congestion. Furthermore Chen and Spector (1992) suggested that the experience of frustration in the workplace can correlate with aggression by employees. As this suggestion has implications for police work we will return to this issue later.

One of the problems with the frustration-aggression hypothesis is that in its original form, frustration was defined in such a wide and general way that it could subsume a whole host of precipitating factors of aggression. More recent research (see Geen, 2001: 22) has tried to separate out some of these and has identified a number of different sets of factors that would fall within Dollard's original and somewhat liberal conception of frustration

Berkowitz (1989) offered a reformulation of the original frustration-aggression hypothesis. He suggested that frustration generally leads to a heightened state of arousal, but when in this heightened state, the person may or may not behave aggressively. Berkowitz suggested that the increased arousal produces a readiness for aggression, but that a number of other factors will determine whether or not the individual chooses to behave aggressively on this occasion. Some relevant factors would include the person's previous experience of this type of encounter, and the situational pressures that are present. Let us consider an example. A young man is waiting to buy a drink at a busy bar. As he is about to be served someone pushes in front of him and gets served immediately. The person who has lost his place will be likely to feel frustrated, will probably become aroused or angry, and perhaps threaten the other person physically. However, in deciding how to react the person may consider things such as the size and appearance of the other person, whether he is with a large group of friends etc. He may also think back to what happened on previous occasions when he challenged someone in this way. Only then will the person decide whether aggression is an appropriate response.

In the light of Berkowitz's commentary it is perhaps best to think of the frustration-aggression hypothesis as a theory of frustration-arousal-aggression. Geen (2001) suggests that the reaction to frustration may in fact be part of a more general tendency to react to changes in our situation. As such, Geen (2001: 26) suggests that:

> Any significant change for the worse in a person's situation may be sufficiently aversive to cause stress and arousal, and that the arousal thus engendered may activate and energise aggressive responses.

Such a notion provides an interesting alternative to the original hypothesis that tried to link frustration and aggression more than 60 years ago.

Before moving on from a discussion of frustration it is perhaps important to note how the frustration-aggression hypothesis differs from those views expressed by Freud and the sociobiologists. Whereas the latter see aggression as a naturally occurring, innate tendency, the frustration-aggression hypothesis posits that aggression will occur only when it is invoked by some external factor: in this case frustration. One might even want to suggest that if there were no frustration, there would be no aggression. Of course the complete removal of frustration is an unattainable goal. However, if there are opportunities to reduce the amount of frustration that people experience then this could have the effect of reducing aggression. Traffic schemes that reduce the amount of congestion might be one example. However, many other sources of frustration (e.g. mass redundancy, lack of promotion opportunities) could not be solved quite so easily.

It was noted earlier that one problem with the original version of the frustration-aggression hypothesis was that its conception of frustration was so ambiguous that it could encompass a whole range of situations, each of which might have its own distinct characteristics. Almost any event that prevents us from carrying on our normal level of activity could be classed as a frustration source. In this case, irritation, distraction, helplessness etc. might all be considered as 'frustrations' according to Dollard's original definition of the term. However, these days, psychologists would be interested in studying the characteristics of each type of situation rather than considering frustration *per se*.

We should note that the frustration-aggression hypothesis still serves a useful purpose as it encourages us to look for features of the external environment that may have an effect on levels of aggression. By doing this we go beyond the simplistic conclusion that people behave violently simply because they are violent people. Consideration of external factors may thus make it more likely that we will make a situational rather than a dispositional attribution when explaining aggressive behaviour (see Chapter 2). This change in emphasis can be important as it forces us to consider a host of external factors that may have at least contributed to an aggressive outburst. Environmental stressors such as heat, overcrowding, noise and air pollution may all have an effect on levels of aggression (Ainsworth, 1995: 95). One of the characteristics of environmental stressors is that they interfere with some ongoing human activity. For this reason it might be important to consider these factors in any discussion of frustration and its possible link with aggression.

Aggression as a learned response – social learning theory

In the previous section it was suggested that a person may or may not behave aggressively in response to frustration and that such a decision will depend partly upon the individual's previous learning experiences. However, social learning theorists have gone further than this in suggesting that the very act of behaving aggressively may be a direct consequence of having observed others behaving in this manner. At its most basic, social learning theory postulates that as people grow up they learn what is and what is not 'appropriate' behaviour. The young boy who observes his father settling even minor disputes by resorting to the use of force may grow up believing that this is entirely appropriate behaviour. If he is also raised on a diet of violent films and television programmes, the belief may become even further ingrained.

Much work on social learning theory stems from a classic study by Albert Bandura (1973). Bandura had two groups of children each watch an adult playing with a large inflatable 'Bobo' doll. For one group of children, the adult was seen to be playing with the doll in a fun, but non-violent way. For the other group of children, the adult model behaved in a much more aggressive manner, kicking and hitting the doll and adding insulting comments as he did so. The children were then given an opportunity to play with the doll and their behaviour was observed. As one might predict, the children who observed the violent model were significantly more likely to behave in a violent way themselves.

Social learning theory has undergone a number of revisions since its original formulation. However, its emphasis on the role of the environment as both a teacher and maintainer of certain behaviours remains. More recently there has been an increased emphasis on the consequences that aggressive behaviour may have for an individual. For example, if a young boy observes an older brother getting what he wants by threatening other children with violence, he may be likely to imitate such behaviour. By contrast if the boy sees an older brother being punished severely for having behaved in a violent way, the child is less likely to engage in this type of behaviour. Thus the child may or may not choose to imitate the aggressive behaviour, the decision being contingent upon the perceived consequences. If the child imitates the aggressive behaviour and either gains materially from doing so, or is praised by others for his actions, then the behaviour is likely to be repeated.

Bandura (1986) has suggested more recently that aggression might be seen in terms of the *values* and *expectancies* that this type of behaviour has for the individual. The adolescent girl who induces fear in her peers by intimidation might learn that bullying behaviour can produce considerable benefits. In this way the perceived value of this type of behaviour will increase. Similarly if the girl's past experience has taught her that she is unlikely to be caught or punished for this type of behaviour, her expectation is that her habits will go unchallenged in the future.

This and other more recent developments of social learning theory have taken us away from the somewhat simplistic notion implied in the original version of the theory, i.e. that children will imitate the behaviour of others. When growing up, children will be exposed to a large number of models and it would be impossible for them to imitate each and every one. However, the child may choose to imitate certain behaviours if it is felt that in doing so he/she may gain some form of reward and avoid punishment. This fact is often forgotten in the eagerness to blame violent television and videos for the amount of aggression in society. According to what Bandura suggests, the television role model who is shown benefiting from aggressive behaviour represents more of a problem than the 'hero' who is shown being punished for his violent conduct. Similarly, new recruits to the police service who observe their older colleagues assaulting or bullying suspects in order to extract a confession will be likely to imitate this form of behaviour, provided that it achieves the desired effect, and the officers are not punished.

There is little doubt that social learning does play a significant role in the acquisition of aggressive behaviour. However, most commentators would today suggest that it should not be seen as the only relevant factor. Whilst having dismissed earlier some of the more extreme claims of people such as Freud, it may not be appropriate to discount completely the notion that we have, in our make-up, the propensity for aggressive behaviour. A combination of genetic factors along with upbringing, social learning, feelings of frustration and the current environmental conditions may all have a part to play in explaining why a person behaved in an aggressive manner on any particular occasion.

The youth who gets involved in a fight as the pubs are closing every Saturday night may be doing so because of a combination of individual and situational elements. If we said that he was behaving the way he was because he is 'that sort of person' we would need to explain why he did not get involved in fights for the other 167 hours of the week. On the other hand if we put forward the view that it is the situation that best explains his actions we would need to explain why millions of other people who visit pubs on a Saturday night do not get involved in fights.

Attitudes towards different forms of aggression

One point that we must bear in mind when discussing violence and aggression is society's attitude towards different types of such behaviour. Many of the examples used in this chapter relate to what might be thought of as typical or representative examples of aggressive behaviour. The fight that breaks out as crowds are leaving bars and clubs is perhaps so 'typical' that it might even be considered a cliché. But of course violence and aggression take many different forms and evoke different responses from society. As noted earlier, society sanctions and even rewards certain forms of aggression. The successful professional boxer or the linebacker who succeeds in injuring the opposing team's quarterback will receive praise, prestige and financial reward for behaviour that may see them sent to prison if carried out in a different context.

There are situations in which our attitude to the type of aggressive act may differ according to the victim and the circumstances. For example, some men may feel that while it is 'okay' to punch another man, it would be something altogether different if the other person were a woman. Having said that, some men may feel that, whilst assaulting a woman would generally be considered inappropriate, if the woman is one's wife it is somehow more 'acceptable'. Interestingly as this book is being finalised, Lennox Lewis, the heavyweight boxing champion is appearing in advertisements designed to reduce domestic assaults. In the advertisements, Lewis makes the point that while his aggression is generally controlled, he may lose his control if he hears about a man assaulting a woman. The intended message presumably is that domestic assaults are unacceptable, though the hidden message (that wife-beaters might get beaten up themselves) is surely inappropriate.

In recent years attitudes towards domestic violence have shown a considerable shift. Not so long ago, police officers would be disinclined to take action against perpetrators of minor domestic assaults. However, more recently, a change in attitude has meant that this type of assailant is much more likely to be charged with an offence. This is borne out by the statistics on domestic assaults that appear to show a large increase over the last 20 years (Ainsworth, 2000: 18). Such large increases in the recorded levels of this type of crime may be accounted for partly by the changing attitudes and policies of law enforcement agencies.

Schonborn (2001) provides an interesting example of how different police forces respond differently to domestic violence. He makes a comparison between the police in Oakland (California, USA) and a Southern Division of the Greater Manchester Police (UK). These two areas were chosen partly because they have similar features in terms of population, number of police officers etc. Schonborn found that the Oakland police arrested 77% more people for domestic violence than did the officers in South Manchester. A number of reasons are offered for this discrepancy including the fact that Oakland officers receive more training in dealing with this type of incident. Also of relevance is the fact that the Oakland police department operate a 'zero tolerance' policy in respect of domestic violence, a move prompted partly by publicity about domestic violence following the O.J. Simpson case in America.

Since 1990 the British police have been mandated by the Home Office to develop proactive policies and operational interventions in respect of domestic violence. This has certainly produced some shift in policy although, as Schonborn found, the message appears not necessarily to have got through to the officers on the street. Hammer and Griffiths (2000) provide an interesting review of successful interventions in domestic violence cases and make a number of recommendations as to how this type of incident might be better policed. They suggest that good policing practice includes:

- standardised definitions of domestic violence and repeat victimisation

- consistent interventions

- organisation and management based on good leadership, accountability and management support

- training of all police staff on domestic violence awareness, good practice and new initiatives

- performance monitoring of officers and forces in terms of attendance and use of resources.

It remains to be seen whether the greater emphasis on domestic violence will continue and whether it will lead to less tolerance, and presumably more arrests in the UK. For a victim, being assaulted may be equally physically and emotionally damaging whether perpetrated by a stranger or a partner. Yet there may remain a view in some police officers that domestic assaults are somehow less warranting of intervention than some other types of violent incidents.

Violence by police officers

Thus far this chapter has looked at some theories of aggression and how the police might deal with such incidents. While the police have to deal with violence and aggression on a daily basis, there will be understandable concern if it is the police themselves who commit such acts. Interestingly police officers are one of the few groups who are empowered by the state to use force, if this is warranted by the particular situation. Police officers may use their batons, CS/pepper spray or in some cases their firearms if this is warranted. However, accusations of police brutality may be made if their actions are considered excessive. The maxim is that police officers should use only 'as much force as is absolutely necessary' in order to effect an arrest or to prevent further crimes being committed. However, the judgement as to what is and what is not 'excessive' force is a difficult one to make. Police officers and their victims will inevitably have different views as to what constitutes legitimate force and whether any particular police action was justified.

In an interesting paper, Chen and Spector (1992) examined some of the factors that might lead to interpersonal aggression amongst a sample of white-collar workers. Although this research did not study police officers, the findings may have some relevance to police work. Chen and Spector found that a number of work related stressors were associated with increased levels of interpersonal aggression. These were:

- role ambiguity
- role conflict
- interpersonal conflict
- situational constraints.

Much of the literature on police stress has pointed to the presence of these factors which appear to be central elements of police work (see Chapter 8). Thus if we are to accept the findings of Chen and Spector's work, we may have some insight into the reasons why some police officers may react aggressively in certain situations. We should also remember that police officers will experience frustrations in the same way as any other occupational group and may react to such frustration in angry or aggressive way.

There will also be other elements of police work that may make it more likely that police officers will behave aggressively. One of the reasons that people have become concerned about the levels of violence on television is the belief that watching a great deal of violence will result in our becoming desensitised to violence itself (Belson, 1979). Not only will we be less likely to react to 'just another' violent incident, we may also become desensitised to the point where we lose our inhibitions about committing violence ourselves. Police officers who deal with violence on a daily basis may, as a result, have fewer qualms about exhibiting the same type of behaviour as many of those with whom they must deal.

Some interesting observations in respect of police use of force are offered in a recent edited publication entitled *Police Violence* (Geller and Toch, 1996). In this volume is an eclectic collection of articles dealing with this complex issue. In an interesting first chapter Klockars grapples with the thorny question of how we should define what is meant by 'excessive force'. He suggests that some of the traditional measures of assessing whether or not the force used was 'reasonable' raise more problems than they solve. He advocates instead that:

> Excessive force should be defined as the use of more force than a highly skilled police officer would find necessary to use in that particular situation.
>
> (Klockars, 1996: 8)

This is an interesting notion albeit one that might prove difficult to apply in practice. However, the definition does encourage us to focus on the officer and his/her level of training and skill rather than simply looking at the outcome of the officer's actions. Thus an officer who shoots a suspect may be judged not to have used excessive force, whereas one who merely handles a suspect roughly may be judged to have done so.

There is no doubt that there are a large number of factors that can conspire together to make it more or less likely that a police officer will behave aggressively. Some of these are to do with the sort of person the individual is while others are to do with aspects of the job, and the types of incidents with which police officers must deal. When looking for an explanation for police violence much of the general research on aggression can be applied to police officers. However, some of the more specialised literature also offers valuable insights. As with other areas of psychological study, understanding of the issues is the starting point. Better understanding of the issues allows us to offer suggestions as to how problems might be addressed and change introduced (see, for example, Kemshall and Pritchard, 1999).

Summary

In this chapter we have seen that a number of factors are relevant to our understanding of aggression, but that no single theory can account for much of the violence witnessed in society today. As Geen (2001: 6) observes 'The alleged causes of human aggression tend to be varied and complex, and discussions of them are most often inconclusive'. Nevertheless the knowledge gained to date helps us to build up a much better picture of aggression and its causes than might a casual observation of the phenomenon. Research has suggested a large number of factors that can be associated with aggression, and only some of these have been addressed in this chapter. We have not attempted to provide a comprehensive review of all possible factors. Some influences (e.g. alcohol and other drugs) have not been considered but the reader may wish to follow up some of the suggestions for further reading listed below.

An understanding of some of the major relevant factors can but help police officers in their dealings with the violent members of our society. Understanding may also help some police officers to come to terms with their own tendencies to behave aggressively.

Further reading

Geen, R. G. (2001) *Human Aggression* (2nd ed). Buckingham: Open University Press.

Geller, W. A. and Toch, H. (1996) *Police Violence: Understanding and Controlling Police Abuse of Force*. New Haven: Yale University Press.

Schonborn, K. (2001) *Policing Society: A Comparative Look at Violence, the Use of Force and Other Issues in the US and the UK*. Duboque, Iowa: Kendall/ Hunt.

Chapter 5

Perception and memory

.

In Chapter 1 we looked at the way in which we perceive other people and examined some of the clues that we attend to when forming an impression of others. Person perception is one example of the way in which we process stimuli from the outside world and use this information in order to form an impression. But the process of perception is involved in far more situations than simply the processing of information about other people. Every time a witness or a victim gives information to a police officer they will be relying on their perception and memory to provide a picture of the event. The police officer will also be relying on his/her perception of the witness before forming an impression of the usefulness of the information that they provide. In this chapter we will consider what psychologists have learned about perception and memory and look at the ways in which a knowledge of these processes will be of benefit to police officers.

Does perception work like a video camera?

It is easy to think of the processes of perception and memory as being similar to a video camera and recorder. When using a video camera we simply point the camera at the scene that we wish to record, press the record button, and the image is imprinted onto the videotape. The videotape can then be stored for days, months or even years and will remain unchanged until such time as we wish to play back the recorded image. Providing the tape has not been damaged in any way, what we view at a later point in time will be an almost perfect copy of what was viewed originally.

In some ways, perception and memory might be thought to mirror this process. After all, the witness to a bank robbery or other crime will have taken in the details at the time of the incident, stored the information for however long was necessary, and then 'replayed' the memory when asked for a statement, or when required to give evidence in court. The criminal justice system tends to perpetuate the view that witnesses are capable of performing such feats, and rarely stops to question whether eyewitnesses are the true reporters of 'facts' that we might assume. Many trials involve the introduction of a great deal of evidence that a jury may have to consider when trying to reach a verdict. But whatever evidence is introduced, a jury is likely to be influenced by a credible and confident eyewitness who asserts that the person in the dock did indeed commit the acts of which they now stand accused.

Does the criminal justice system have unrealistic expectations of eyewitnesses?

The role of witnesses is crucial to many investigations. Prosecutors may decide that it is not even worth taking a case to court if there are no independent witnesses who can support the charges against an accused. However, whilst the criminal justice system may come to rely heavily upon the information provided by eyewitnesses, the system may have unrealistic expectations as to the ability of eyewitnesses to provide objective and accurate information (Ainsworth, 1998a). If perception and memory really did work like a video camera and recorder, there would be little problem. Indeed with the increasing use of CCTV, many criminal acts will be caught on videotape and the court will be able to see for itself that the accused did commit the crimes of which they are accused. However, in the absence of such 'hard' evidence the story of an eyewitness will often be viewed as the next best thing. The testimony of an eyewitness, especially one who is credible and confident, would appear to come second only to a confession by the accused in terms of its influence on a jury (Wakefield and Underwager, 1998: 423).

How does perception work?

In order to understand why the video camera analogy is inappropriate we will need to consider how perception works. One immediate barrier to understanding is that perception is a process that we employ continually yet rarely stop to consider how it works. At this moment in time, your eyes will be taking in the information provided by the words on this page. But the eyes themselves will not be imposing meaning on what are in effect a series of different shaped black lines on a white background. In order for you to make any sense of these stimuli, your perceptual processes will need to translate the shapes and interpret them correctly. Providing that your eyesight is reasonable and that you have a good knowledge of the English language, this should present few problems. However, if you stop to think about what is being achieved here it is actually a very complex skill. One can see this as a four-stage process. i.e.:

1. The black lines need to be recognised as letters.

2. The letters need to be recognised as forming words.

3. The words need to be recognised as words and their meaning understood.

4. You need to understand what the writer actually means when he/she uses the words in a certain combination.

Most people would have little difficulty with the first three of these stages, and would invariably agree on what was before them. However, the fourth stage allows for far more in the way of subjectivity and interpretation. If, for example, you were asked to summarise what you have read in this chapter so far, what you produce would not necessarily be identical to what another person would produce. Your interpretation of what you have read would essentially be subjective and allow a large number of perceptual biases to come into play. If, for example, you are reading this simply because you find the subject of perception and psychology interesting, your overall impression of the points made here may be positive. On the other hand if you have been required to read this chapter because it is part of the set reading for some course or other, your overall perception may be somewhat more negative and quite different. If you and your colleagues are required to write an essay based on the contents of this chapter, it is unlikely that any two people will produce an identical essay. Each person will have taken slightly different points from this chapter, perhaps interpreted them slightly differently, and made a different decision as to what points should be included in an essay about perception.

Perception as a learned process

The point about perception is that it is not a static, objective process that simply takes in what is given. Rather it relies to a large extent on trying to provide the best interpretation of the information entering the sense organs. In many cases the interpretation may be correct and we never even give it a second thought. However, in some cases the information can be interpreted in a number of different ways and it is not quite so obvious what the 'correct' interpretation should be. If you are travelling in an aeroplane at 30,000 feet, a glance out of the window may suggest that you appear to be moving very slowly – the horizon rarely changes and the clouds pass by at a leisurely pace. However, you may be aware that the plane is in fact travelling at over 500 mph and that your original interpretation of the stimuli entering your sense organs is inaccurate. Similarly if you are sitting in a traffic jam and see the car alongside you apparently rolling backwards, it may not be obvious whether your interpretation of the visual stimuli is correct. For example, if the car next to you was stationary and it was your own vehicle that was moving forwards, the visual information provided to you would be virtually identical.

One of the best ways that the process of perception can be demonstrated is by examining the Necker cube.

Figure 5.1: The Necker Cube.

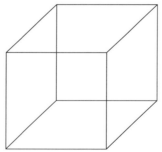

What is in front of you is a two-dimensional representation suggesting a three-dimensional object – in this case a cube. If you stare at the cube for a few moments you may notice that it appears to 'reverse' and that the face that was first presumed to be at the front now appears to be at the back. The reason why the figure has this ability to reverse is that the lines can be interpreted in one of two different ways, and, in this case there is no 'right' answer. Because this is so, our perception shifts its interpretation first offering us one and then the other possibility.

Perception as a constructive process

Perception has been compared to the testing of a hypothesis (Gregory, 1980). Our perception suggests one hypothesis as to what any stimuli might 'mean' and we can either accept or reject the hypothesis. In the case of the Necker cube, there are two alternative, competing hypotheses for us to consider. Because we are unable to say that one hypothesis is correct and the other incorrect, we are unable to accept one and reject the other. Most people report that, even if they try to stop their perception switching to the alternative, they are unable to do so.

The view of perception that is being suggested here is known as the *constructivist* approach. Its best known proponents are Richard Gregory and Ulrich Neisser (Gregory, 1980; Neisser, 1967). The approach rests on a number of assumptions including:

- Perception is an active and a constructive process.

- Perception is the end product of the interaction between the stimuli themselves and internal factors such as hypotheses, knowledge, and motivational and emotional factors.

- Our hypotheses and expectations are prone to error and, as a result, our perception may be biased and inaccurate.

Thus, as we have seen in this chapter so far, the perception of stimuli goes far beyond the simple 'reading' of what is out there. Eysenck (2001: 27) summarises the viewpoint thus:

> The frequently inadequate information supplied to the sense organs is used as the basis for making inferences or forming hypotheses about the external environment.

Given this view it is difficult to imagine any form of perception that would not require some involvement from our accumulated knowledge. Newborn babies have few hypotheses about how the world might be perceived, but over time each individual builds up a store of knowledge that helps them to interpret the world. Without such experience, perception would be very difficult. For example when looking at an object going away from you, the pure visual information would suggest that the object decreases in size as it moves away. However, your accumulated knowledge of the world tells you that this phenomenon is in fact a type of visual illusion and that the object does not in reality become smaller as it moves into the distance. This can, however, lead to some interesting errors in perception. Look at Figure 5.2 below.

Figure 5.2: Line illusion

If one looks at the two horizontal lines it appears that one is longer than the other. This is, however, an illusion as the two lines are identical in length. In this case our perception is being led by the two other lines that converge towards the top. These two lines might be interpreted as something going away from us. We know that if we look at railway lines going into the distance they appear to get closer together – however, our experience tells us that this is in itself an illusion and the lines remain the same distance apart. In Figure 5.2, our perception suggests that as the two converging lines appear to be going into the distance, the horizontal line nearer the top should appear to be smaller. Because it does not conform to this rule we perceive it as being longer. This could have implications for eyewitness testimony. A witness who is asked about the height or build of an assailant may have difficulty in providing an accurate estimate, especially if the person is some distance away.

In order to make sense of stimuli, perception will, if necessary try to fill in any gaps in the information. Thus if you look at Figure 5.3 below you will tend to perceive this as a circle with a section missing.

Figure 5.3: A circle?

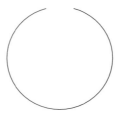

Your perception will try to make the best guess as to what this might represent and mentally fill in the missing part that would make it into a circle. If we had never seen a circle before, however, we may well not perceive it in this way. This tendency to 'fill in' any missing information can have implications for the testimony that witnesses provide. If a witness's perception is incomplete initially they may tend to fill in any missing details by working out what probably happened. The problem then is that when they come to give a statement it will not be immediately obvious which parts are based on what was actually seen or heard, and which bits have been added by their perception.

This tendency is illustrated even more clearly by Figure 5.4. Here you are asked to say how many triangles there are.

Figure 5.4: Triangle illusion

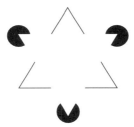

The chances are that you will have reported seeing two triangles, i.e. one black one with the point at the top, and one white one with the point at the bottom. If it was suggested to you that the white triangle did not actually exist you would probably not agree. It seems 'obvious' that the white triangle is there as one can see its entire outline. However, if you try covering up the three incomplete black circles the white triangle disappears. So how does this illusion work? When our perception is faced with the information in this figure, it tries to make the best bet as to what it represents. In this case the best way of interpreting the incomplete circles and the black-lined triangle with parts missing is to imagine that there is a white triangle placed on top of the black lines and shapes. So strong is our tendency to do this that the 'imagined' white triangle is perceived as an actual triangle.

Here again there are obvious implications for the way in which witnesses take in information about things that they see. Witnesses may well produce a story based on what they perceived, but this may not necessarily be factually correct. Those who believe in the existence of the Loch Ness monster may be convinced that the dark shape visible on the horizon is that of the infamous Nessie. Those with a little more scepticism may view the same shape very differently.

Inaccuracies and biases in perception

The problem with accumulating experience about the world is that in building up a knowledge base, inaccuracies and biases can be incorporated within the perceptual process itself. Thus to return to a theme introduced in Chapter 2, an individual who is prejudiced and routinely stereotypes members of another group will tend not to perceive any actions committed by members of that group objectively or dispassionately. This was illustrated convincingly in an experiment carried out by Duncan (1976).

Duncan's study concerned the perceptions of actions committed by members of one's own race and the actions committed by members of another race. He initially made a film that depicted two people arguing. The argument became somewhat heated and in the end one person was seen to push the other. Duncan made two slightly different versions of the film: in one the 'aggressor' was shown to be a white male whereas in the other he was a black male. In both cases the 'victim' who was pushed was a white male. The two different versions of the video were shown to two separate groups of white American college students.

After viewing the video the two groups were questioned about what they had seen. The students were asked to categorise the behaviour of the aggressor and included in the categories were terms such as 'playing around' and 'violent behaviour'. The categories chosen by the participants appeared to be heavily influenced by the race of the aggressor. When he was black, some 70% chose to categorise his behaviour as 'violent behaviour', whereas when the aggressor was white only 13% of participants chose this category. The two versions of the video were virtually identical except for the fact that the race of the perpetrator was varied. This variance would, however, appear to have led to completely different perceptions on the part of the observers (who were in this case all white).

If these results can be extrapolated to the world outside the laboratory, they would appear to have quite serious implications. The actions of people on the streets may be judged not simply on the basis of their inherent qualities but also on the basis of the background of the perpetrator. In this case, not only may victims and witnesses perceive actions differently on the basis of the race of the offender, but the judgements of police officers might also be affected.

The effects of context

One aspect that can sometimes help our perception is the context in which some stimuli or other appears. Thus a series of loud bangs may be interpreted as fireworks or as gunfire, depending on the context in which people find themselves. If we see a man breathing heavily and sweating profusely, the fact that he is wearing a running vest and shorts may help us to understand why he is displaying these signs. However, an individual exhibiting the same behaviour when dressed in dark clothing at 1am may well be viewed with more suspicion.

You may want to try looking at the following list and saying the words out loud.

Chair   Stool   Seat   Bench

Nothing difficult there of course, as all the words are recognised easily and the third word is easily perceived as a seat. Now look (or have a friend look) at the following list and say the four words.

Audi   Volvo   Seat   Subaru

The chances are that in this case the third word would be perceived as being the name of a car company based in Spain. Note that the two words' visual appearance is identical and yet our perception recognises the different contexts in which each appears and then makes the best guess as to what the word should be. Of course this only works if one is familiar with the names of car manufacturers. However, there are many other words in the English language in which the pronunciation and meaning is entirely dependent upon the context in which the word appears. For example the word 'staple' can be used in the sense of something that holds together pieces of paper or in the sense of a 'staple diet'. Few people would perceive the latter term to refer to a meal that consisted entirely of small pieces of metal.

Knowing the importance that context can play in perception alerts us to errors that may affect the accuracy of eyewitness accounts. For example, a mugger who threatens a hapless victim may be perceived as extremely threatening and be remembered as being taller than they were in reality. Context allows us to go beyond the information contained in the stimulus itself and can be an aid to perception. However, context can also distort perception and lead us to misinterpret information. For example, the bank robber's getaway car may be perceived as being driven faster than was actually the case, because one presumes that in that context the robbers would want to leave the scene as quickly as possible.

Selectivity and perception

Perception is, by necessity, selective. Humans are incapable of attending to and processing a large number of different types of information at any one time. For this reason witnesses may be able to provide quite detailed information about some aspects of an incident while having virtually no memory for other aspects. In general people attend to the most vivid or most demanding aspects of a scene whilst ignoring other less interesting aspects. Thus witnesses may have quite good recall for the actions of a bank robber whilst in the bank, but may be able to offer less information about the appearance of the person. One consequence of this tendency to be selective in perception is that victims may be able to provide a detailed description of the weapon used by an assailant but can say little about the person's face. This tendency has been referred to as *weapon focus* (Loftus *et al*, 1987; Steblay, 1992; Pickel, 1998).

If one couples the tendency for perception to be selective with the tendency for witnesses to make systematic errors in the perceptual process, we can see that information given by eyewitnesses should always be treated with a degree of caution. Errors of omission (i.e. where a witness simply fails to mention a possibly important detail) can be frustrating for the police. However, of more concern should be errors of commission, in which a witness gives the police unreliable information, simply because of the way in which perception works.

Memory – storing and retrieving information

Perception can be considered as the first stage in the memory process. As such it is often referred to as the encoding stage – information is encoded before being placed in the memory store. As we have seen above, perception is the point at which we interpret and try to make sense of the incoming information before passing it on to the other stages of the memory process. The next two stages involve the storing and subsequent retrieval of information.

We argued above that the view of perception as being like a video camera was inappropriate. It is also inappropriate to view the rest of the memory process as being identical to a video recorder. Far from being a permanent record that is immune to interference and confusion, a great deal can happen to information once it has been put into the memory store. Not only can information be transformed but we can also experience considerable difficulty when we try to retrieve the stored information. We will address some of these points in what follows.

The transformation of memories

Another analogy that is sometimes used to illustrate how memory might work is that it is like a filing cabinet. According to this viewpoint, each new memory is stored in a file within our filing cabinet and remains there until such time as we wish to access the information again. When we do so, we extract the appropriate file, open up the contents and are then able to reproduce the original memory. However, this view of memory is not supported by psychological research. In particular the belief that information lies dormant and unchanged within the memory store may be inappropriate. Research by people such as Loftus (1979) has investigated this.

Loftus set out to examine whether it was possible to manipulate people's memories. Many of her studies involved showing people films or a series of slides depicting incidents such as a car accident and then asking a number of questions about what had been shown. She would typically include a piece of misleading information amongst these questions and then test the memories of her 'witnesses' a week or so later. Typical of this approach was one study in which people watched a film in which a car was seen to drive along a country road and was then involved in an accident (Loftus, 1975). When questioned shortly afterwards, some viewers were asked a deliberately misleading question, i.e. 'How fast was the car going when it passed the barn on the country road?'. In reality there was no barn, however, when questioned some days later, 17% of people claimed to have 'seen' the non-existent barn.

A similar study involved showing a series of slides depicting a car accident. (Loftus *et al*, 1978) After viewing the slides, the participants in the study were asked a number of questions about the incident. Embedded within these questions was one that was deliberately misleading in that it gave false information about the type of road sign that was shown at the junction. A week later, those who had seen the original series of slides were invited back and asked to indicate what type of sign they had seen at the junction. Of those who had been given the misleading information almost 60% got the answer wrong, apparently having been confused by the misleading information. (This compares with only 25% of people who gave the wrong answer when no misleading information was introduced.)

What studies of this type suggest is that memories do not lie dormant until such time as recall is needed. Rather, the research suggests that memories can be altered, especially by misleading information that is introduced shortly after something has been witnessed. Even if an interviewer encourages a witness to try to retrieve the original memory, they may still inadvertently produce a contaminated version and be unaware that their memory is not accurate.

One point of interest in many of the Loftus studies is the fact that misleading information can be effective even if it is introduced via a different sense modality than that via which the original information was taken in. This suggests that there are not separate memory 'stores' for different types of information, but rather that any information about a particular incident may be stored in the same 'place' irrespective of the source of that information.

There is some debate in the psychological literature as to whether the original memory has been 'overwritten' by the new memory or whether the original is still in the memory system but difficult to access (Ainsworth, 1998a: 58). For present purposes this debate is not particularly important – if the end result is that a witness is unable to retrieve an original memory when asked to do so, it matters little whether or not the original memory does still exist. Even if it could be proved that the original memory was still lodged within the memory somewhere, unless it can be retrieved it is of little value to the police.

It appears that confusion arises mainly because of problems in source monitoring. Misleading information causes confusion and witnesses incorrectly come to believe that the source of the information is the original incident rather than the subsequent misleading information. As a result witnesses experience source misattribution. In one interesting study, participants in a misinformation experiment were asked if they would be prepared to bet money on their ability to recover an original memory (Weingardt et al, 1994). Most were prepared to do so, yet they still invariably made mistakes and produced contaminated memories.

Another of Loftus's studies showed that in some cases the introduction of misleading information can lead to what has been called a compromise memory (Loftus, 1977). In this study, participants were shown a series of slides, one of which showed a green car driving past the scene of an accident. However, some of the participants were then asked a misleading question which suggested that the car was blue. The participants were later questioned about the colour of the car and a number of people picked out a blue-green shade that resembled turquoise.

This finding is particularly interesting as it suggests that, rather then one memory being replaced by the other, the two pieces of information were somehow fused together and the end result was a compromise between the colours blue and green. This could have consequences for the questioning of witnesses. For example, a witness to a car accident might have as their original memory that one vehicle was travelling at about 30mph. However, if it is suggested to them that the car may have been travelling at 40mph, they may eventually come to believe that the actual speed was 35mph, this being a compromise between the two pieces of information.

For the purposes of policing, the results of these types of study appear to have quite far reaching implications. The stories that witnesses tell will tend not to be a simple recall of original memories but will be a mixture of original memories and any subsequent information. It might be argued that Loftus's work, while interesting, is largely irrelevant, as police officers would never deliberately introduce misleading information when interviewing witnesses. They may, however, do this inadvertently by for example letting the witness know what other people have said about the incident. Misleading information may also have been introduced by other people to whom the witness has spoken, or even by reports in the media. For this reason, it is important to acknowledge that a witness's statement may be an amalgamation of what was seen originally and what has subsequently been gleaned about the incident. When we add to this equation the fact that witnesses will tend to be biased in the way in which they take in and process information in the first place, it would be unusual for any witness to be capable of producing a complete and objective account of an incident.

The importance of question wording

Even if interviewers are careful to avoid asking leading or suggestive questions, the exact wording of the questions might still have an effect. For example, a police officer investigating a car-pedestrian accident might ask a witness how *far away* a vehicle was when the pedestrian stepped into the roadway. Alternatively the officer might ask *how close* the vehicle was when the pedestrian stepped out. Neither of these would be judged to be leading questions, yet the subtle difference in wording might lead to a different estimate of distance. This could be important. For example, if the police officer makes a judgement that the car driver had ample room to stop but did not do so, a prosecution may follow. On the other hand if the officer decides that the motorist had little time to react and could not have avoided a collision with the pedestrian, it is unlikely that any action will be taken.

The importance of question wording was investigated in another Loftus study (Loftus and Palmer, 1974). In this case 'witnesses' were shown a film depicting an accident between two cars and then asked a number of questions about the incident. Amongst the questions was one that asked 'How fast was the car going when it hit the other vehicle?'. However five different groups of people who had seen the accident were asked the question in a slightly different way. Thus although the first group were asked about the speed when one 'hit' the other, other groups were asked about the speed when the vehicles 'smashed', 'contacted', 'collided' or 'bumped' into each other. Each of these different forms of the question elicited a slightly different average estimate of speed. However, the largest difference was found when the words 'contacted' and 'smashed' were used. In the former case, the average speed was almost 31mph, whereas in the latter it was nearly 41mph. This is a large difference that appears to emanate entirely from the way in which the questions were asked. There is no suggestion that any of the questions were 'leading' yet they appeared to have a dramatic effect on the answers given.

In an interesting follow on from this study, Loftus and Palmer had their 'witnesses' return to the laboratory some time later and they were questioned further about what they had seen. One question asked about whether the subjects had seen any broken glass at the scene of the accident. Of those witnesses who had been asked about cars having 'hit' each other, 14% claimed to have seen broken glass. However, of those who had been asked about cars 'smashing' into each other, over 30% claimed to have seen broken glass. In reality no broken glass was shown at the scene, yet as these results show, almost one third of those who had been asked about cars smashing into each other claimed to have seen broken glass.

It is easy to see why this might have occurred. If people had a memory of cars having 'smashed' into each other it would be reasonable to expect that there would have been broken glass. In this case, expectation may well have played a part and the witnesses based their answer on this, rather than on what they had actually witnessed. Once again we can see how difficult it appears to be for some witnesses to go back to an original memory and ignore any subsequent information. The memory does not sit undisturbed as it would if it were on videotape. While the memory may well fade with time, it might also become distorted, have sections removed or new sections inserted. In this way it may perhaps be better to think of memory as being like the information obtained when using a digital camera. Such information can be downloaded onto a computer and manipulated as one likes. As such 'images' can be altered and the eventual output be considerably different from what went into the camera originally.

Is alteration of memories more likely in certain circumstances?

Before moving on from this consideration of the work of Loftus we should perhaps note that in none of the studies conducted to date has it proved possible to alter the memories of *all* those who took part. Although it is possible to demonstrate that alteration can occur it is not always possible to explain why some people retain their original memory whilst others are affected by the manipulation. Research suggests that alteration is more likely under the following conditions:

- When the person does not immediately detect a discrepancy between post-event information and an original memory (Hall *et al*, 1984).

- When the introduction of post-event information restores memory for the original incident to an 'active' status (Hall *et al*, 1984).

- When the misleading information is introduced shortly before memory is tested (Loftus *et al*, 1978).

- When the detail to be altered is peripheral rather than central to the incident that is witnessed (Loftus, 1979)

However, even taking these factors into account it is still not possible to predict with certainty which witnesses will be affected and which will not. Even the somewhat common sense viewpoint that confidence is linked with accuracy has rarely been supported by research (Loftus, 1979: 101). For this reason, some psychologists (e.g. Cutler and Penrod, 1995) have argued that courts should be made aware of the difficulties faced when trying to evaluate the likely accuracy of eyewitness testimony.

We should note that, although the studies discussed above relate to memory for events, Loftus has demonstrated that memory for facial details can also be altered. For example in one study (Loftus and Greene, 1980) participants were instructed to look at a face and then some time later to try to recall details of the face. However, in the intervening period, some subjects were given misleading information about some aspect of the face (e.g. that the hair was curly when it was in fact straight). In this case, those who had been given the misleading information were significantly more likely to be incorrect in their recall of the original feature.

Factors that might affect witnesses at the time of recall

In the sections above we have suggested that memories can be affected both at the time that information is taken in and while the memory is in storage. Research also suggests that there are factors that will affect witnesses at the time that they are asked to recall details of the incident. We will be dealing with the recovery of memories in some detail in the next chapter, but it is important that we are aware of some of the variables that can affect recall at this stage.

One obvious factor is anxiety. If a witness is particularly nervous they may find it difficult both to take in and to recall information accurately. For most victims and witnesses, giving evidence in court will be a stressful experience. Not only might they be recalling information about a particularly harrowing ordeal, they will also find themselves in an alien environment where the 'rules' are very different from anything they might have experienced previously. Courts rarely take steps to make a witness's ordeal less traumatic and, as a result, recall may suffer. There is some evidence to suggest that stress can interfere with recall when a witness is attending an identification parade (Ainsworth and King, 1988). It seems reasonable to presume that the levels of stress experienced when giving testimony may be even greater.

Summary

In this chapter we have seen that perception and memory are complex processes. We have seen that there is far more to these processes than an analogy with a video camera and recorder might suggest. Perception relies on a large number of factors, each of which may have the effect of distorting the view of reality that people take in. Attitudes and stereotypes held by a witness can mean that a large amount of what is perceived may be inaccurate and biased. Far from being seen as passive and objective, perception is perhaps best viewed as a personal and subjective process that colours what we attend to and how we interpret it.

Even if information is perceived accurately it is still possible that the memory can be altered through the introduction of misleading questions or even by the way in which questions are worded. Until such time as interviews with witnesses are routinely recorded we can only speculate as to how the final written version of a witness or victim's statement has been arrived at. Police officers should be aware of the fragility of human memory and how their own actions can affect what a witness produces (Wright *et al*, 2000). This is a theme that will be developed in the next chapter.

Much of what psychologists have discovered about perception and memory has real implications for police work. If police officers are made aware of these findings, it is hoped that a better evaluation of the real value of eyewitness evidence will be forthcoming (Kebbell and Wagstaff, 1999).

Further reading

Ainsworth, P. B. (1998) *Psychology, Law and Eyewitness Testimony.* Chichester: Wiley.

Eysenck, M. W. (2001) *Principles of Cognitive Psychology* (2nd ed). Hove: Psychology Press Ltd.

Kebbell, M. R. and Wagstaff, G. F. (1999) *Face Value? Evaluating the Accuracy of Eyewitness Information.* PRCU Police Research Series Paper 102. London: Home Office.

Chapter 6

Retrieving information

In the previous chapter we looked at the areas of perception and memory and considered how the knowledge gained from psychology could help our understanding of these processes. It was suggested that the criminal justice system may have unrealistic expectations as to the ability of eyewitnesses to produce accurate and objective accounts of incidents that they have witnessed. Having said that it also appears that there are some techniques that can be used with witnesses to help to recover information from the memory system. In this chapter we will consider two possible ways in which witness recall might be improved, i.e. the use of the cognitive interview technique, and the use of investigative hypnosis.

The cognitive interview technique (CIT)

The cognitive interview technique provides one of the best examples of the way in which psychology and policing can be brought together productively. The technique was devised by two American psychologists, Ronald P. Fisher and R. Edward Geiselman, almost 20 years ago. Since its introduction it has undergone some modifications but has now been adopted by police forces in a number of different countries. It introduces concepts from both cognitive and social psychology and attempts to provide police officers with a range of skills and techniques that can help witnesses to remember as much detail as possible about an incident.

The importance of witness interviewing

Police forces have traditionally devoted considerable time and effort in training their officers to interview suspects, but have often failed to spend an equivalent amount of time teaching officers how to obtain information from witnesses and victims. Where training was given in respect of such interviewing, it was generally concerned with ensuring that officers produced statements that would be acceptable to the court rather than with using techniques that might aid witness recall (Stewart, 1985). Sanders (1986) reported that 98% of US police officers received no training in witness interviewing. In the UK George (1991) reported that there was considerable variation between police forces in respect of witness interviewing. However, six forces reported having no formal training and 10 offered training of less than one day.

Ede and Shepherd (1997) suggest that to many police officers a 'good' statement is one that is chronological, plausible, non-contradictory, confirms other evidence, and addresses the points that need to be proved in any offence. As a result, what little training is devoted to witness interviewing fails to emphasise the importance of appropriate retrieval techniques. The division between suspect interviewing and witness/victim interviewing is found in the psychological literature although the reader should note that at least in the UK both are subsumed under the title of *Investigative Interviewing* (Milne and Bull, 1999).

This situation with regard to witness/victim interviewing may appear somewhat surprising. After all the police are more likely to be able to identify a suspect if they have been given a good deal of accurate information about the crime and the perpetrator. Indeed one of the best predictors of whether or not a crime will be solved is the quality of the information supplied by witnesses and victims (Rand Corporation, 1975). However, for many years the police appear to have believed that whether or not witnesses came up with 'good' information was almost a matter of chance – some crimes threw up good witnesses who would help to identify a perpetrator and some did not. The idea that the police might be able to improve the amount of information that each witness was able to produce was, until relatively recently, anathema.

Acceptance of techniques such as the cognitive interview

The reluctance even to consider that 'outsiders' may be able to offer advice and assistance in this area is not untypical of organisations that have a high degree of ethnocentrism (Ainsworth, 1995: 69). Within the police service there is often a feeling that the people best qualified to train and educate new officers are those who have themselves gained considerable practical experience of the job of policing (see Chapter 3). It is rare for any police-training establishment to employ more than a handful of trainers who do not have practical experience of policing. The problem with this approach is that there is likely to be little impetus to introduce change to the curriculum, and new officers are given little opportunity to consider techniques or ideas that might originate from outside the walls of the establishment. For any change to be introduced there will need to be considerable impetus from both outside and inside the organisation. If imposed upon the service, any change may be unlikely to succeed if those within the job do not believe that it will have benefits for officers themselves.

Given this tendency, the adoption of techniques such as the CIT has not always been straightforward. In the case of the CIT, Fisher and Geiselman were able to demonstrate its effectiveness both in the laboratory and in the field and it was this that persuaded some police forces to adopt its use. In what follows we will discuss some of the important points covered by both the original CIT and the revised (or enhanced) cognitive interview.

The interview as a social interaction

Fisher and Geiselman's starting point was to look at the way in which witnesses have traditionally been interviewed by the police. They noted that rarely did police officers try to use any techniques that would help the witness to recall more detail. In fact, it was suggested that the 'typical' interview with a witness may well have had the opposite of the desired effect and might discourage the witness from trying to recall as much information as possible. One example of this was research by Fisher *et al* (1987) that showed that, rather than allowing witnesses to tell their story in their own time, police officers would typically interrupt the witness within seconds of their having started to speak, thus breaking their concentration.

Perhaps the first point to note about the witness interview is that, like many other situations, it involves a social interaction. In this particular case the two participants in the interaction have different roles to play, although they may ultimately wish to achieve the same result, i.e. the identification of a perpetrator. For the police officer the interview may be a necessary but not particularly exciting part of the job. Because police officers are involved in the taking of statements almost every day it is easy to forget that for the victim or witness this will be far from an everyday occurrence. If the person to be interviewed is the victim, they will probably have already suffered the trauma of victimisation and are now being asked to do something that may be novel and possibly daunting. If the interviewee is an uninvolved witness they may still feel somewhat uneasy about the situation. The chances are that they will have little experience of this type of interview and so will rely on the police officer to put them at ease and to treat them with respect. While victims will generally be highly motivated and want to do all they can to help the police they may still have a 'fear of failure' and will want to try to do well. The uninvolved witness may not have the same fears, but may be wondering whether they have done the right thing and may be concerned about the possibility of having to appear in court at a later date.

Shifting power from interviewer to witness

The point is that both victims and witnesses will have reason to feel uneasy about this type of interaction and will rely on the interviewing officer to establish the ground rules as to what will happen. Traditionally, police officers in this situation would have taken charge and would have directed the witness as to how they should behave. Cast in this role, the witness is in a position of powerlessness and will probably become passive and submissive to the directions of the officer. As a result, a statement may be produced that satisfies the needs of the officer in terms of format etc., but in which there is little detail (Ainsworth, 1995: 22). One of the first points to note about the cognitive interview (especially in its revised form) is that it seeks to reverse this situation and to put the witness in the dominant role. This may appear to be a subtle shift, although it represents a considerable switch of roles for the police officer. Police work often involves directing members of the public to behave in certain ways. In many situations to which the police are called, those present at the scene will look to the officer for advice and guidance as to what they should do. As a result, the handing over of control to the witness may not come naturally for many police officers. This is a point that is explored further in Chapter 10.

Fisher and Geiselman suggest that by putting the witness in the dominant role they are more likely to participate actively in the interaction. Consequently they may be less likely to be led by the interviewer and more able to give an uncontaminated version of the incident (see Chapter 5). The officer should thus encourage the witness initially to relate their story without interruption. Whilst doing this, the officer should adopt an active listening style that communicates to the witness that what they are saying is of interest to the officer. If an officer expresses his/her disappointment at the scant detail provided initially, the witness may feel much less motivated to try to help the officer further. By contrast, the attentive interviewer who smiles, encourages and thanks the witness throughout the interview process is more likely to motivate the witness to try hard to recall more detail. Furthermore, the witness will leave the interview room feeling that their contribution has been valued and that it was worth the time and effort expended in helping the police in this way.

Encouraging the witness to talk

There are a number of ways in which a police officer can encourage the witness to say more. For example, asking open-ended questions from the outset will establish a pattern of responding in which detailed answers are encouraged. By contrast, an officer who starts by asking closed questions (i.e. those to which a simple Yes or No answer can be given) will communicate to the witness that detail is not necessary. If the interviewee is a victim who has been traumatised by their ordeal, the officer should be sensitive to this fact and spend some time establishing a rapport with the person. Communicating empathy will help the victim to feel more comfortable and let them know that their difficulty is understood. By contrast, an officer who expresses impatience towards the victim may alienate the person and make them less likely to want to help.

Although the officer may see the situation as 'just another interview', it will generally be helpful if some attempt is made to personalise the interview. This can be as simple as the using of first names, or asking initially about the witness's interests or hobbies. The reason why such details are important is that a witness who has already built up a good relationship with the interviewing officer will be more highly motivated to want to help the officer. In some cases a good relationship is more likely if interviewer and interviewee are similar in terms of age and sex. It will for example be much more difficult for a male officer to build up a good relationship and express empathy with a female victim of rape. Another way in which rapport can be built up is by self-disclosure on the part of the interviewer. Police officers may be reluctant to divulge personal information to a witness, but anything that allows the witness to see the police officer as a person rather than just someone in a uniform will help.

During the interview, officers should try to avoid making judgements about what is being said and should avoid confrontation with the witness. When there appear to be discrepancies in what a witness says, the officer should hold back from pointing these out until the witness has finished speaking. In general the pattern to be adopted will be to ask the witness to give a 'free recall' without interruption and then to ask specific questions about the incident. Psychological research suggests that when asked to provide a free recall, witnesses do not produce a great deal of information, but what is produced is generally accurate. By comparison, under direct questioning, witnesses will provide more information, but a higher proportion of this will be inaccurate (Lipton, 1977).

When asking direct questions it is still important that the interviewer avoids passing judgement on the information, at least at the time that it is given. Once again a witness who is made to feel uncomfortable will be less likely to want to help the interviewing officer. Officers should bear in mind many of the points made in Chapter 5 of this volume and not presume that the witness can simply replay the video recording inside their head and produce a clear and concise picture of events. Patient probing will often help the witness to clarify details whereas accusing the witness of incompetence will tend to have the opposite effect.

Much of what has been said so far is concerned with verbal communication. However, as we saw in Chapter 1, a great deal of social interaction is governed by effective non-verbal communication. The witness will tend to notice a look of impatience or a glance of incredulity on the face of the interviewing officer and may respond to these irrespective of what the officer is saying. The officer can also communicate concern and empathy non-verbally and can provide a model of calm behaviour with which the witness can identify. Anxious witnesses and victims will tend to speak quickly and in doing so may omit important detail. An officer who can encourage the witness to mirror his/her own relaxed conversational style is likely to elicit far more detail. In a similar vein it is important that the officer tries to eliminate unnecessary interruptions and distractions. The sound of a personal radio constantly emitting garbled messages will do little to help a witness to concentrate. Such sounds may also communicate to the witness that the officer is very busy and that the witness should not take up any more of his/her time than is absolutely necessary.

The social interaction that takes place within the interview situation should be born in mind throughout the process. Although we have concentrated mainly upon strategies that can be used at the beginning of an interview, many of the points are relevant throughout the interview itself. For example, an interviewer may build up a good rapport at the start of the session but this can diminish as the witness starts to relate details of what may have been a particularly stressful experience. As a result, the officer should be prepared to pause at any time and allow a good relationship to be re-established. When the interview is over, the interviewer should also make an effort to thank and to reassure the witness. A witness who goes away feeling that they have been a failure in some way will have a negative view of the interview and perhaps also of the police in general. Even a witness who was not able to provide a great deal of useful information will still have given up their time in an effort to help. This fact should be remembered even if the officer feels frustrated by the fact that little of value has been gleaned.

The mechanics of the CIT

Having considered some of the ways in which the interview itself might be managed, we will now look at some of the more important aspects of the CIT itself. The original version emphasised four main components, i.e. *recreating the context*, *focused concentration*, *multiple retrieval attempts*, and *varied retrieval*.

Recreating the context

The CIT draws on psychological research in suggesting that a witness will tend to remember more if they can recreate the original context during which they witnessed the incident. Rather than starting the interview by inviting witnesses to tell their story 'cold' it may be of benefit to encourage them to think about the circumstances surrounding their presence at the scene. Thus the witness might be encouraged to say what they were doing in the bank when the robbery started, whether they were in a hurry, whether they were feeling hassled or what they were thinking about generally. Fisher and Geiselman believed that the more the witness can recreate the original context, the more they are likely to remember. Each additional piece of 'context reinstatement' may provide additional retrieval cues that may help the witness to provide more detail. For example, a witness may remember that they were in a hurry because they had left their car parked on a double yellow line outside the bank. This may trigger a memory that the witness thought initially that one of the robbers was simply trying to push in the queue and that she had said something to him about this. This in turn may allow the witness to recall something about the voice of the robber.

Recreating the context appears to be quite effective in that witnesses do recall additional information when invited to do this. If you have ever had the experience of going into a room and then forgetting what you went in for, you may have tried going out of the room again in the hope that this will trigger the memory. This is similar to context reinstatement in that, by putting yourself back into the environment where the thought originated, you are more likely to connect to the thought. In some ways, context reinstatement may achieve a similar effect as taking the witness back to the scene and having them describe what occurred there. Doing this provides additional retrieval cues for the witness and may also allow them to demonstrate actions that they have difficulty putting into words.

Whilst the originators of the CIT did not advocate taking a witness back to the scene, doing so may have a similar effect to mental context reinstatement. However, there might be problems associated with a witness returning to the scene. Apart from issues of practicality, the witness may for example become more anxious if asked to return to the scene of a harrowing incident. In addition, whilst returning to the scene would certainly reinstate the physical context, it may do little by way of helping the witness reinstate the mental context (e.g. how they were feeling, what they were thinking etc).

Focused concentration

Remembering can be a complex cognitive task requiring considerable mental effort. Most people will be used to telling stories or recounting witty anecdotes, but they will rarely have been asked to try to remember a great deal of detail about a specific incident. If witnesses are to produce a large amount of information then this will require considerable mental effort on their part. The best way in which this might be achieved is by concentration on the matter in hand. Consequently the interviewer will need to encourage the witness to think long and hard about different aspects of the incident. After allowing for a free recall of information, the interviewer might ask the witness to think about one particular aspect (e.g. the appearance of one of the perpetrators) and to focus on that exclusively. If the witness remembers something about the gun that one of the robbers was holding, the witness might be instructed to think about the gun and then to think about the hand that was holding the gun. For example, the witness might be asked whether the robber wore gloves. If not, they may be asked whether the robber was wearing rings or asked whether the fingernails were neatly manicured or bitten.

Much of this technique is based on the belief that a witness holds a great deal of information within the memory system, but that they will need to focus and to concentrate very hard if they are to retrieve much of the detail. Instructing the witness to pay close attention to the more detailed sensory representations that are held within the memory system is likely to produce beneficial results. The interviewer must, however, be aware that any interruptions to this task can break concentration and leave the witness floundering.

Multiple retrieval attempts

In the previous section it was suggested that a witness may hold more information within their memory store than they can access at any given time. For this reason the CIT advocates that the witness should be encouraged to make more than one attempt to retrieve information from their memory. Key to this is the belief that a witness may be able to retrieve different information at different times or in different ways. Care should, however, be exercised here. An interviewer who pushes a witness more and more despite their having said that they have no memory for a particular detail may persuade the witness to invent a detail that is plausible but for which no actual memory exists. We saw in Chapter 5 that witnesses may tend to fill in any gaps in their memory and that they are more likely to do this if bullied into providing some kind of answer. It may not be obvious to the interviewer that this new 'information' is simply confabulation. For this reason, witnesses should only be persuaded to make further attempts if it seems obvious that they are experiencing a temporary difficulty in retrieving a particular item.

Bearing this proviso in mind, there may be benefit in asking the witness to make further retrieval attempts, especially if they feel that the information required was in their memory once, but it is not accessible at this point in time. It is perhaps inappropriate to see memory as an 'all or nothing' phenomenon i.e. that the information either is or is not in the memory store. The reality is perhaps best illustrated by the so called 'tip-of-the-tongue' phenomenon (Brown and McNeil, 1966). This is the state in which a person knows that they know the answer to a question but is unable to vocalise it at that particular point in time. It is an odd state in that the person often claims to be able to identify the first letter of the word, and even how many letters it contains, yet cannot come up with the word itself (Levelt *et al*, 1999). In some cases, witnesses may say that they tried to memorise some detail (e.g. the registration number of a getaway car) but that it seems to have 'gone' now. In cases such as these, multiple retrieval attempts may be of benefit, especially if they suggest alternative ways of accessing the memory for a particular detail. Thus in the example of the 'lost' registration number, the witness might be asked about how they had tried to remember it, and then to work from there.

Varied retrieval

Witnesses will generally give their own version of events in a chronological order and from their own perspective. However, in the original version of the CIT, Fisher and Geiselman advocated that witnesses should be asked to recall the details again but in a different order, or from a different perspective. Thus witnesses might be asked to recount the events from the moment the robbers left the bank, working backwards to when they first entered. Perhaps surprisingly, this technique can be effective and such attempts often produce additional information (Geiselman *et al*, 1986).

The other suggestion (that the witness might tell the story again but from the perspective of someone else at the scene) is perhaps more controversial. Whilst it is acknowledged that witnesses will tend to tell their story from the perspective of how it affected them, it will be difficult for them to produce additional information by talking about what other people 'might' have seen. Although Fisher and Geiselman warned of the dangers of using this instruction to witnesses, it is fraught with danger. A witness who has built up a good relationship with an interviewer will want to do all they can to help the person. As such they may be tempted to 'invent' detail in order to try to please the interviewer. Most people will not find it easy to tell their story from the perspective of someone else at the scene – they can really only imagine what someone else would have seen and in these circumstances, information provided will tend to come from the witness's imagination rather than their memory.

As noted above, the varied retrieval technique was played down in the revised version of the CIT (Fisher *et al*, 1987). However, other related techniques may be of value. For example, although witnesses will describe primarily what they saw, being asked to consider other sense modalities might be of benefit. Thus asking specifically about a perpetrator's voice may trigger a memory regarding an accent or speech impediment. If a witness has come into close contact with an assailant, they may remember that they had rough hands, or that they suffered badly from halitosis. Such information might be valuable in itself, but it can also trigger other memories that might be of more obvious benefit to the police.

Evaluation and implementation of the CIT

The vast majority of studies that have looked into the effectiveness of the CIT have concluded that it produces more information than does a more traditional form of witness interviewing. There is, however, some debate over which parts of the CIT are the most useful and whether all components are necessary in order to produce enhanced recall (Ainsworth, 1998a: 108). In a recent meta-analysis of 42 studies, Kohnken *et al* (1999) concluded that the amount of information produced by both the original and the revised version of the CIT was significantly greater than that typically obtained in a standard interview procedure. Most research has found that the increased amount of information that is retrieved is accurate, although some studies did show a slight increase in the amount of incorrect information produced. Nevertheless, the proportion of accurate to inaccurate information was roughly similar. Kohnken *et al* (1999) found that on average 85% of the information retrieved using the CIT was accurate compared with 82% for the non-cognitive interview.

However, the story does not, unfortunately, end there. One might naïvely presume that, if a technique was as successful as the research suggests, it would be welcomed by the police and used routinely. This appears not to be the case, at least in the UK. While almost all police officers in the UK will have received some training in the CIT, many do not use it routinely. There appears to be a perception that the CIT is more time consuming than a traditional interview, and, when dealing with day-to-day volume crime, the extra time and effort is simply not worthwhile (Kebbell *et al*, 1999). As a result, the CIT appears much more likely to be used by seasoned detectives when investigating the more serious types of crime (Croft, 1995).

Croft suggests that officers may be reluctant to use the technique with traumatised witnesses and victims. A proportion of police officers appear to feel that some of the instructions contained within the CIT might re-traumatise the witness by having them relive their experience in a vivid way. At present it is difficult to say whether these officers' concerns are justified. Milne and Bull (1999: 50) make the point that, for some victims, being able to tell their story in detail may be an important first step in coming to terms with their victimisation. Nevertheless, police officers may have concerns over using any technique that might make the interviewing of an already traumatised victim potentially more stressful. Such concerns are not limited to the taking of statements by police officers (Ainsworth and May, 1996).

In a recent evaluation of investigative interviewing in England (Clarke and Milne, 2001) a rather disappointing picture of witness interviewing emerged. In this survey some 58 interviews concerning volume crime and 17 concerning serious crime (murder) were evaluated. The report's executive summary states that:

> The overall standard of these interviews was poor with no evidence of the techniques for enhancing witness recall being used....The volume crime interviews were in fact statement taking exercises and not interviews at all. (p. ii.)

This viewpoint is reiterated later in the report, its authors noting that only one quarter of the time that officers spent talking to witnesses and victims was taken up with interviewing – the remaining three quarters was spent in writing out the statement. The research found that, in more than half the cases, interviewers never or hardly ever used questions appropriately. Given this information it is perhaps unsurprising that the researchers report that less than one third of the interviews were judged to have provided a comprehensive account of an incident. The problem is encapsulated in the following statement:

The whole process seems to have been dominated by a sense of haste rather than an (increasingly rare) opportunity for the police to obtain information which may prove to be valuable in the prosecution (or elimination from an enquiry) of persons suspected of a crime.

(Clarke and Milne, 2001: 105)

The report did acknowledge that where more time was afforded to officers (e.g. in the investigation of the more serious cases) the interviews were generally of a higher standard. Nevertheless it is disappointing that an interview strategy that was adopted by all police forces and in which almost all officers have received some training resulted in so little change in practice. Some of the possible reasons for this have been discussed above. However, the report by Clarke and Milne also makes the important point that 'it is difficult to convince police managers of the value of interview training, in part because there is currently no method of measuring its impact on performance' (p. iii.). For this reason it is recommended that appropriate performance indicators be developed in order that the impact of interviewing can be measured. Nevertheless it may still prove difficult to persuade those working within a pressured police service that the additional time and effort that the CIT is believed to involve is worthwhile.

Hypnosis

Another method that has been advocated as a means of extracting more information from victims and witnesses is the use of hypnosis. As with the CIT, one of the beliefs that underlies the use of hypnosis is that witnesses have far more information within their memory system than they can access at any one time. Allied to this is the belief that in some cases witnesses and victims who have been badly traumatised by their ordeal may experience difficulty in recalling some of the details. When in a 'normal' state such people might find that to re-live the experience would be very painful and disturbing, whereas when under hypnosis, recall might be easier. Some of those who advocate the use of hypnosis also claim that particularly traumatic memories might become repressed and be pushed into the unconscious mind. Access to these memories will then only become possible through techniques such as hypnosis. We will consider these points in what follows.

Widespread interest in the possible use of hypnosis stemmed from a number of cases in which it appeared that the technique had had remarkable success (Reisser, 1989). Perhaps best known among these was the Chowchilla kidnapping case in the USA. This took place in 1976 when a group of 26 children on a school bus were kidnapped and held in a quarry near Chowchilla, California. The children were eventually released unharmed although the police had little initial success in identifying the perpetrators. The driver of the bus on which the children were travelling then agreed to be hypnotised, and whilst under hypnosis was able to provide part of the registration number of the vehicle used by the kidnappers. This information allowed the police to identify those responsible for the crime and they were subsequently convicted of the kidnapping. As news of this and other cases spread, police forces throughout the world showed an interest in the use of hypnosis and many tried the technique for themselves. Martin Reisser (then a psychologist with the Los Angeles Police Department) set up courses in which large numbers of police officers were trained in the use of investigative hypnosis.

However, as more and more people started to employ hypnosis, a number of psychologists became concerned about its use. One of the foremost critics was Martin Orne (1984) although others expressed similar concerns (Wagstaff, 1993; McConkey; and Sheehan, 1995). The problem arose not so much from the use of hypnosis itself, but more from the way in which it was being used. Providing that its use was confined to the providing of leads that the police could then investigate, there were few concerns. However, problems could arise when the police took what witnesses said under hypnosis as 'fact' and presumed that it must be true. There were even more concerns over cases where witnesses who had been hypnotised were later asked to give evidence in court. We will consider these concerns firstly by looking at the nature of hypnosis itself.

The hypnotic interview

There is some debate over the nature of the hypnotic state itself. Some people see it as a state of consciousness separate from the normal waking and sleeping state, whilst others do not see it in this way. However, most writers agree that a number of changes do occur within the person under hypnosis. These can be summarised as follows:

- The person will be more relaxed when under hypnosis and will suspend or at least lower their normal critical judgement. As a result they may say things of which they are unsure or which they would not think of saying when not under hypnosis.

- The person will be more compliant when under hypnosis and will want to do what they can to please the hypnotist. As a result they may comply with the hypnotist's request for more information even if they do not have an actual memory upon which to draw.

- When under hypnosis the person will be much more suggestible and will pick up on any cues given by the hypnotist. As a result leading questions may have an even more dramatic effect than when used on non-hypnotised subjects (see Chapter 5). The hypnotist's influence on the subject may not be so obvious but nevertheless be effective. For example, a suggestion that the subject is 'doing really well' may be perceived as meaning that they have come up with the 'right' answer even though such an answer may be a result of confabulation.

As mentioned above, these points may not necessarily cause undue problems providing that information obtained under hypnosis is treated just like any other 'lead' and investigated by the police. However, if the information is presumed to be factual and the witness then appears in court there are clear dangers. For example, a witness who confabulates (i.e. fills in details by speculating about what might have happened) may come to incorporate the confabulated detail into what they believe is their original memory for the event. This may be a particular problem if, when under hypnosis, the subject is told that when they awake they will remember everything that has been said during the session. Such an instruction may have the effect of convincing the hypnotised person that all the details are correct and repeating them in court under oath will pose no problem.

It would be naïve to presume that a witness will be able to separate out detail from their original memory from that which originated from speculation or suggestion. We saw in Chapter 5 how susceptible non-hypnotised witnesses can be to post-event misleading information. In the hypnotic state (in which the witness is both more compliant and more suggestible) the problem is compounded.

There are other potential difficulties that have been identified by writers such as Orne. One of these is a concern over who should conduct the hypnotic interview. As mentioned above, Martin Reisser routinely trained police officers in the use of investigative hypnosis and saw no problem with such individuals conducting the hypnotic sessions. However, the primary motivations of police officers will generally be to solve the case as quickly as possible and, as a result, they may not be unduly concerned about the welfare of the witness. If, for example, a witness becomes extremely distressed during a hypnotic interview, the police officer may be reluctant to break off the session and will be ill-equipped to offer help or counselling to the person. Another concern is over the fact that the police officer may be tempted to 'lead' a witness, especially if those working on the case have already made a judgement as to who may have committed the crime. Even a police officer who is careful to avoid using leading questions may still inadvertently cue the witness by the way in which they ask questions or by the way in which they respond to any information that a witness provides.

As a result of these and other concerns, writers such as Orne have suggested that it may be inappropriate for previously hypnotised witnesses to give evidence in court. Predominant among the reasons for this assertion is that the witness will be unable to distinguish original memories from those that have been confabulated or that have arisen as a result of suggestions or comments made during the hypnotic interview. Although it might be argued that the court itself should be able to make a judgement about such matters, the reality is that it is very difficult to identify which memories are genuine and original, and which are not. A further problem that Orne identifies is that a previously hypnotised witness will appear more certain of the 'facts' than might someone who has not undergone such a procedure. This can pose difficulties for not only are members of a jury more likely to believe a confident witness, but such a person may also be virtually immune to the normal challenges that might emerge under cross examination.

These and other concerns have prompted a number of states in the USA to prohibit previously hypnotised witnesses from giving evidence in court. Other states within the US allow such witnesses to give evidence, but only if a number of important safeguards have been implemented. These include such things as the complete video recording of the hypnotic interview. This allows the court to be able to decide for itself whether a witness was unduly pressured or led during the session. Such video recording also allows the court to consider whether the techniques that a hypnotist has used were appropriate. For example, a hypnotist might suggest to a witness that, although the suspect was 50 metres away, they have a pair of binoculars that they can use to get a better look at the person and describe him/her. If the suspect really was so far away that the witness could not possibly have seen any facial details, no amount of encouragement from the hypnotist will be able to retrieve a 'memory' that never existed in the first place.

It would thus appear that while some gains may emerge as a result of the use of hypnosis, there are a number of concerns and costs that must be balanced against these. Hypnosis may be appropriate with victims and witnesses who have suffered a great deal of trauma and who, for whatever reason, are unable to recall much detail about their ordeal. In such cases the problem can lie with the retrieval process itself rather than with the fact that the witness has little memory for what occurred. However, even in these cases, the information that does emerge should still be treated with scepticism and should not be presumed to be accurate unless or until other corroborating evidence can be found. In a recent article, Loftus (2001) argues that people can experience difficulty in separating out 'real' memories from those of events that have been imagined or which are based on stories told by others. It would appear that when hypnosis is used, the chances of such confusions may be even greater.

Summary

In this chapter we have looked at two techniques that appear capable of improving the amount of information that can be obtained from witnesses and victims. In the case of the cognitive interview technique, this is a procedure that was first developed by psychologists and appears to offer considerable potential. Providing that the procedure is taught and used correctly, it can lead to an increase in the amount of information typically produced by witnesses. That this is achieved largely without a subsequent increase in the amount of incorrect information is commendable. However, we also saw in this chapter than unless procedures such as the CIT are embraced fully by both managers and practitioners within police organisations it is unlikely that their potential will be realised.

With regard to the use of hypnotic interviews it has been argued that the widespread use of such techniques may not be appropriate. As we saw in this chapter there are a number of very real concerns over the quality and value of information obtained under hypnosis. Unlike the CIT, hypnotic interviews have considerable potential to increase the amount of incorrect information that a witness produces. Where such techniques are used, there are a number of important safeguards that must be incorporated into the procedure. Even where such safeguards are accepted there will remain a concern over the appearance in court of a witness or victim who has previously undergone a hypnotic interview. If non-hypnotised witnesses are as vulnerable to misleading information as the research covered in Chapter 5 suggests, we should perhaps be even more concerned as to the reliability of information obtained whilst witnesses are in a more relaxed, compliant and suggestible state.

Further reading

Heaton-Armstrong, A., Shepherd, E. and Wolchover, D. (1999) *Analysing Witness Testimony: A Guide for Practitioners and Other Professionals.* London: Blackstone Press.

McConkey, K. M. and Sheehan, P. W. (1995) *Hypnosis, Memory and Behaviour in Criminal Investigation.* New York: Guildford Press.

Milne, R. and Bull, R. (1999) *Investigative Interviewing: Psychology and Practice.* Chichester: Wiley.

Chapter 7

Interviewing suspects

In Chapter 6 we looked at some ways in which witnesses and victims might be interviewed. The other form of interviewing in which police officers will be involved routinely is the interviewing of those suspected of having committed criminal offences. Television dramas often portray the interviewing of a suspect in a dramatic way, suggesting that persuading a reluctant suspect to confess is a skill possessed by only a small number of seasoned officers. Within the police organisation itself, an officer who is able to 'crack' a case by obtaining a confession may be held in high regard. As with other topics explored in this book so far, suspect interviewing is an area in which the application of findings from psychological research may be appropriate. In this chapter we will look at appropriate and inappropriate interviewing techniques and address the thorny issue of false confessions. We will also look at the detection of deception and assess the extent to which police officers may be good at spotting when a suspect is lying.

Investigative interviewing

In Chapter 6 we noted that there have recently been attempts in the UK to link both the interviewing of suspects and the interviewing of witnesses/victims under the same umbrella (Milne and Bull, 1999). Although we will be treating the two separately in this volume we will briefly consider some of the relevant features of investigative interviewing and the way that it might affect the interviewing of suspects.

Training in investigative interviewing was introduced in the UK following research that unearthed some quite serious problems with police officers' interviewing skills (Baldwin, 1992). This research pointed to a number of concerns including lack of preparation, ineptitude, poor techniques and presumptions of guilt. Subsequent to this research and following concerns over a number of false convictions, training in investigative interviewing and the PEACE training package was introduced. Investigative interviewing was based on a number of principles including:

1. The role of investigative interviewing is to obtain accurate and reliable information from suspects, witnesses and victims.

2. Investigative interviewing should be approached with an open mind.

3. When questioning anyone, the officer must act fairly.

4. Police officers do not have to accept the first answer given – questioning can be persistent but still fair.

5. The police still have the right to put questions to a suspect even when their right to silence is exercised.

6. Police officers are free to ask questions in order to establish the truth.

7. Vulnerable victims, witnesses and suspects must be treated with particular consideration.

(National Crime Faculty, 1996: 18)

These principles formed the basis for interview training and the introduction of the PEACE training package. PEACE was an acronym for a five-step process that provides an interview structure, i.e.:

Planning and preparation
Engage and explain
Account
Closure
Evaluation

Each of these stages was itself broken down (see Milne and Bull, 1999 Chapter 9 for a fuller explanation). For example, under the planning and preparation stage are matters such as understanding the purpose of the interview, defining its aims and objectives, analysing the available evidence, assessing what other types of evidence is required, and demonstrating knowledge of PACE (the Police and Criminal Evidence Act, 1984).

The introduction of the PEACE training package was intended to remedy a number of problems with interviewing that had been identified in earlier research (e.g. Baldwin, 1992; Williamson, 1994). Such research had suggested that police officers were sometimes ill prepared, conducted interviews poorly and in some cases breached the requirements of legislation (e.g. PACE). However, perhaps of most concern was the fact that police officers often saw the primary purpose of suspect interviewing as the obtaining of a confession rather than to establish the 'facts' in the case.

Attributions about suspects

If one takes the typical scenario of an interview with a suspect it may be possible to see what attributions might be made. A 'suspect' will tend be interviewed if the police have a reasonable suspicion that the person has committed an offence. The person may have been arrested because they were found near the scene of a crime or because they match the description given by a witness. If the person has previous convictions for the same type of crime, then the police may already have come to believe that the individual is more than likely responsible.

In such circumstances the police may, not unreasonably, approach the interview itself with a belief that the person has committed the offence in question and that the purpose of the interview is simply to persuade him/ her to admit involvement in the crime. The police officer may expect the suspect to deny involvement, at least initially, but such denials may be presumed to stem from the suspect's wish to avoid punishment rather than because they are innocent. One study carried out in the UK (Moston et al, 1992) found that, in over 70% of cases, police interviewers were already 'sure' of the suspect's guilt before the interview began. If the suspect had previous convictions, then the presumption of guilt was even higher. Such presumptions have been supported by other research (e.g. McConville and Hodgson, 1993). Furthermore in almost 80% of cases, interviewers questioned by Moston et al stated that the aim of the interview was, quite simply, to obtain a confession.

If police officers enter the interview situation with these beliefs it is unlikely that they will be focused on other purposes that the interview is supposed to serve, i.e. establishing the true facts in a case and eliminating the innocent (Swanson et al, 1988). Of course if the police do have the correct suspect in the interview room then approaching the interview in this way may not necessarily pose a problem. If there is overwhelming evidence against a suspect then the obtaining of a confession may not be seen as important – the suspect will probably be charged, irrespective of what is said in the interview room. However, in cases where the evidence against an accused may be insufficient to warrant the case going to court, there may be more pressure on the interviewing officer to come up with additional evidence in the form of a confession.

Moston *et al* (1992) found that in cases where the evidence against an accused was only moderately strong, the eliciting of a confession had a marked effect on the outcome. In 87% of the cases in which a suspect did confess, charges were brought, but in those cases in which the suspect did not confess, only 45% were charged. Interestingly, Moston's research also found that suspects who exercised their right to silence during an interview were more likely to be charged than were those who chose to answer questions but denied the offence. (The reader may wish to note that this research was carried out before a change in the wording of the caution that told defendants that it may harm their defence if they fail to mention something that they later rely on in court.)

The 'right to silence' is an interesting issue. Some argue that it is a sacrosanct right that the law should protect, while others say that it stands in the way of police investigations. In fact a number of arguments have been put forward both for and against the 'right' (see for example Leng, 1994; Cherryman and Bull, 2000). One might presume that those who were innocent would want to protest their innocence as much as possible, and to offer an explanation for the police's apparent mistake in suspecting them. One might also presume that those who are guilty and have something to hide would be much more likely to invoke their 'right' and to say nothing until they have had time to think up a 'story'. However, such a viewpoint is perhaps a little naïve and somewhat simplistic. There might be a number of reasons (including some psychological) that a person would choose to say little even if they were innocent. The changing in the wording of the caution does, however, appear to exert more pressure on a suspect to say something, even when it might not be in their best interests to do so. As noted earlier, the police might have their own very firm views as to what a suspect's unwillingness to speak signifies, although it seems likely that not all such refusals will arise simply because of a suspect's guilt.

What is clear from research such as that carried out by Moston *et al* is that police officers may enter the interview situation with certain presumptions as to what is likely to happen. Elsewhere (Ainsworth, 1998b) it has been suggested that there are at least five presumptions, i.e.:

1. Almost all suspects will lie in order to avoid conviction.

2. The vast majority of suspects are 'obviously' guilty, and the purpose of many interrogations is to gain additional information that simply adds to the already 'overwhelming' evidence.

3. Most suspects can be persuaded to admit their guilt eventually. Those who cannot be so persuaded are skilled rather than innocent.

4. Experienced police officers, especially seasoned detectives, are good at persuading reluctant suspects to confess (even allowing for the restrictions imposed by PACE).

5. No suspect who is truly innocent would ever confess.

Whilst some of these presumptions may be appropriate in some circumstances, they do not reflect the 'open mind' with which police officers are now expected to approach the interview situation. The problem with almost any presumption is that it will affect the way in which people process information about others, and the way in which attributions are made about others' behaviour. For this reason, much of the material covered in Chapter 2 appears relevant to the interview situation. If the five presumptions listed above are true, almost anything that the suspect does or says will be interpreted in such a way as to fit the mind-set and presumptions of the interviewing officer. Thus the guilty suspect might be expected to:

- protest their innocence repeatedly

- argue that the police's version of events is inaccurate

- make claims that challenge the 'evidence' that the police have already accumulated

- become more agitated the longer the interview goes on, especially if the police do not appear to believe what the suspect is saying.

These presumptions may appear reasonable, but before accepting them we may wish to pause for a moment and consider how a person who is genuinely innocent might react when brought into the interview room and accused of involvement in what may well be a serious crime. It is possible that the four types of behaviour described above may apply equally to a person who has been wrongly accused of involvement in a crime. In fact if one thinks about how a person might best go about trying to persuade police officers of their innocence, it is difficult to come up with any strategy that could not be presumed to be indicative of guilt as opposed to innocence. For example, a suspect who exercises their right to have a legal representative present during the interview might be presumed to be doing so because they have something to hide rather than because they think that this is the best way to protect themselves from what may be a spurious accusation.

Perhaps the point is that in the interview room as in many other arenas of human interaction, presumptions are made about the meaning that any action signifies. The point was made in Chapter 2 that the world would be a much more difficult place if people did not make some presumptions about others, and did not make use of stereotypes. As with any stereotype, assigning a person to the category of 'suspect' brings with it certain presumptions about how that person is likely to behave and also about how we should attribute a cause to such behaviour. Thus whilst protestations of innocence may be taken at face value so long as a person has not already been categorised in some way or other, once the label 'suspect' is attached, the protestations are evaluated somewhat differently. To bring in concepts introduced in Chapter 2, police officers may make an internal attribution about a suspect's protestations of innocence, whereas they may make an external attribution about the same level of protest emanating from someone who has not yet been so labelled.

Identifying those who are lying

One example of this tendency to presume that suspects are guilty and will invariably lie is provided in an article written by a quite senior British detective (Oxford, 1991). In this piece (entitled *Spotting a Liar*) Oxford claims that 'suspects usually lie in order to avoid guilt or criminal proceedings' (p. 328). It is interesting that in this instance Oxford uses the term 'suspects' rather than perpetrators. He is apparently unconcerned that 'suspects' are, until convicted, those *suspected* of having committed a crime. The article goes on to make a number of other claims about how a lying suspect may give themselves away. For example he states that:

> 'I know what you are saying but...' is another favourite, but an innocent person has no need to show that he understands the question before he gives an answer.
>
> (Oxford, 1991: 328)

Oxford provides no empirical support for his statements, relying instead upon his accumulated experience in the interview room. The problem is of course that we have no way of knowing whether Oxford's beliefs are correct. To the best of the current author's knowledge there is no research that shows that the guilty and innocent would behave differently in this situation.

Other claims made by Oxford also demonstrate the problem with relying upon personal experience and anecdote rather than on well-conducted research. For example he states that:

Both the innocent and the guilty will be nervous, but the guilty person's nervousness is often more physical, reflected in excessive perspiration, nervous laughter, yawns or sighs.

(Oxford, 1991: 329)

Here again it is difficult to judge the accuracy of Oxford's presumptions. Recent publications in the area of lie detection (e.g. Ben-Shakhar and Furedy, 1990; Vrij, 2000) make no reference to the sorts of differences claimed by Oxford. Indeed Vrij (2000: 178) makes the point that an innocent person may experience nervousness/anxiety if they do feel that their truthful statements will not be recognised as accurate. For example, Vrij suggests that, during a polygraph examination, innocents may be wrongly accused of lying because they are not convinced of the polygraph's ability to make an accurate judgement about their answers.

Police officers may come to believe that suspects will invariably lie when interviewed, and that such lies will be easily detected. In some cases (e.g. where the police officer knows that the suspect was at the scene but he/she claims that he was not) the lie will be easily spotted and the suspect confronted. However, in many other cases police officers may make the presumption that a suspect is telling lies by observing their behaviour when in the interview room. As was noted above, such strategies may be unhelpful as it is actually very difficult to establish whether a person is lying or just feeling uncomfortable. Furthermore, even those who are lying may not give off the sorts of non-verbal signals that are presumed to be associated with lying. As Vrij (2000; 51) notes:

Experienced criminals ... or people in the public eye for whom it is important to make a good impression on others ... are unlikely to show nervous behaviour when they are lying.

Vrij makes the point that many of the subjective indicators of deception that people typically use when judging others are not reliable. For example, both police officers and civilians may believe that when a suspect is lying he/she will not be able to make eye contact with the interviewer. As a result it may be presumed that gaze aversion is a good measure of lying behaviour. The research evidence does not, however, offer overwhelming support for this belief. Despite this, Vrij (2000: 78) found that approximately 80% of police officers (including detectives) believed that gaze direction was a good indicator of deception. Gaze aversion is of course quite easily controlled, so anyone who wishes to avoid being branded a liar may make a conscious effort to make eye contact when lying.

In some cases, beliefs about lying behaviour may be the exact opposite of what research suggests. For example, Vrij and Semin (1996) found that police officers typically held the view that lying would be associated with an increase in hand and finger movements. In reality, the exact opposite is more likely to be the case with interviewees showing a decrease in hand and finger movements when lying. Interestingly when Vrij tried to help police officers to spot liars by bringing this fact to their attention, they chose to ignore the advice and fell back on their original beliefs in respect of hand and finger movements. Partly as a result of this, they performed poorly in an experiment that tested their ability to detect deception.

The vast majority of accumulated evidence would suggest that people are not very good at detecting deception and often perform no better than chance when asked to make judgements about the truthfulness of others' statements. Whilst it may be presumed that police officers would be better than the average member of the public at detecting deception there is little evidence to support such a belief. In the vast majority of studies in which police officers have taken part, they have performed no better than non-police officers. In some studies, police officers have even performed at a level below chance (Vrij, 2000). One of the main reasons for this perhaps surprising finding is that police officers tend to make incorrect presumptions about the signals that liars will give off. As a result, attention may be focused upon inappropriate cues whilst other possibly more reliable information is ignored.

Whilst most of the studies do suggest that most police officers perform poorly in lie detection tasks, some studies have found that certain groups of law enforcement personnel may perform better than average. For example, Ekman and O'Sullivan (1991) found that US Secret Service agents performed significantly better than college students in a deception detection test. Ekman et al (1999) also found that some US federal officers with special expertise and experience in the area of deception, and a group of sheriffs who had been identified as being skilled interrogators, did perform better than the average police officer.

In a recent article Vrij (2001: 596) makes an interesting point with regard to police officers' beliefs about their ability to spot liars. He points out that officers who are overly confident about their ability to spot liars will tend to jump to a conclusion quickly and will not bother to scrutinise suspects carefully. Furthermore their misplaced confidence will mean that they consider it unnecessary to try to improve their lie detection techniques. Vrij does, however, accept that it may not be appropriate to extrapolate the results of laboratory-based studies to the detection of deception in many everyday policing situations. Police officers themselves believe that it is easier to spot liars when actively conducting an interview with a suspect than when passively watching a person talking on video. Interestingly, however, this belief is not supported by the evidence currently available (e.g. Granhag and Stromwall, 2001), most of which suggests that it is more difficult to detect deception when conducting an interview than when simply observing another person. Interviewing involves a number of different tasks (e.g. deciding which questions to ask next), each of which will increase the cognitive load of the interviewer. By comparison, the observer can devote all their time to the task of identifying if or when a person is lying.

One interesting recent development in the area of deception detection concerns the possible use of indirect measures of deception. In such studies observers are not asked to try to spot lies as such, but rather to attend to certain features of the speaker and what they are saying. For example, in one study (cited in Vrij, 2001: 598) police officers were asked not to judge directly whether a speaker was lying but rather to assess whether they appeared to be having 'to think hard'. In this case, police officers performed better than would have been expected had they simply been asked to assess whether the speaker was lying. Vrij suggests that there may be some advantage in training police officers to look for such indirect measures of deception rather than have them rely on their stereotypical (but often incorrect) assumptions about the behaviour of liars. Although research in this area is at an early stage, Vrij (2001: 598) suggests that 'using indirect measures to detect deceit has the potential to become a useful tool in lie detection in legal contexts'.

False confessions

One of the main reasons why psychologists have focused on the techniques used in interviews with suspects is the possibility that the interviewing methods that might persuade a guilty person to admit an offence may also lead to an innocent person making a false confession. One immediate problem, however, is that it is very difficult to establish the number of cases in which a false confession is made. Furthermore, as we will see later, there are a number of different types of false confession, some of which occur as a result of coercion on the part of the interviewer(s) and some of which arise as a result of other factors.

Wakefield and Underwager (1998: 425) make a distinction between *false confessions* and *coerced* or *nonvoluntary confessions*. They point out that not all coerced confessions are false, and not all false confessions are coerced. For example, a man may make a voluntary 'confession' in order to protect another family member. Such a confession may be false but not coerced as it was made voluntarily by the person. These problems of definition exacerbate the already difficult problem of establishing what proportion of confessions are false or coerced. Rattner (1998) claimed that in 8.4% of cases of wrongful convictions, a coerced confession was at least partly responsible for the miscarriage of justice. In a survey of prison inmates in Iceland, Gudjonsson and Sigurdsson (1994) found that 12% of prisoners claim to have made a false confession. However, Cassell (1998) suggests that such figures are over-estimates and that false confessions tend only to be made by individuals who have learning difficulties or who have serious mental health problems. The difficulty for any researcher is that many confessions that are claimed to be false or coerced may only be proven to be so if a person has their conviction quashed at a later date. Many others may claim that their confession was false although it will be all but impossible to verify such claims.

Despite the doubts concerning confessions, such evidence can have a great deal of influence on the outcome of a trial. This is still the case even when the reliability of the confession is brought into question. As Wakefield and Underwager (1998: 423) note:

> A confession has a compelling influence on jurors and they are more likely to convict on the basis of a confession than anything else.... This effect persists even when the jury is fully aware that a confession was coerced and likely nonvoluntary.

Such a claim is supported by work such as that conducted by Kassin and Sukel (1997) whose research found that even when a confession was recognised as being coerced and was stricken from the record, mock jurors were still more likely to convict an accused. The mock jurors in this study even claimed that they had not been influenced by the confession despite the fact that the research was able to demonstrate that they were so influenced.

Types of confessions

A number of different types of false or coerced confessions have been identified. These include:

Confession to achieve fame or notoriety. Whenever a particularly serious crime comes to light it is not uncommon for large numbers of individuals to walk into police stations and to claim responsibility for the crime in question. Such individuals may choose this rather unusual behaviour in order to bolster their low self-esteem. In most cases it will be easy for the police to identify this sort of person and not to take their claim seriously.

Confession in order to assuage guilt feelings. Some individuals may harbour guilt feelings about any number of things and believe that they should be punished for whatever they have done. Such feelings of guilt may stem from actual acts or, in some cases, from imagined ones. Claiming that they have committed some crime or other is one way in which the person can receive the punishment that they believe they deserve. This behaviour is most likely in those suffering from some form of mental illness or personality disorder in which feelings of guilt are not uncommon.

Confession in order to protect another individual. Such cases were introduced briefly above. In most cases these will involve one family member lying in order to protect another family member. However, there may be other cases, e.g. where one gang member agrees to 'take the rap' for another member and is then rewarded by the gang for such behaviour. In some cases this apparently altruistic behaviour is voluntary, but in other cases the individual may be threatened that if they refuse to do this, they or members of their family will be harmed. In the latter case, the confession might be regarded as both false and coerced. McCann (1998) has labelled this type of confession *coerced-reactive*. McCann claims that this should be viewed as a distinct type of false confession. In some cases, serious intimidation will be used in order to persuade the confessor to take the blame. As such, McCann argues that the apparently altruistic actions of someone who takes the blame for a crime they know they did not commit may stem not so much from altruism but from fear.

Confessions arising from an individual confusing fantasy with reality. This state is most likely to be encountered in individuals suffering from a psychotic disorder (e.g. schizophrenia) in which the dividing line between fantasy and reality may become blurred. Such individuals may have had fantasies about harming others on a number of occasions and may not realise that such fantasies are fundamentally different from reality. Although such cases are often obvious to the police, for the individuals themselves, the belief that they are guilty may be firmly held and they may become frustrated by the fact that their confession is not taken seriously.

Coerced confessions arising from pressure exerted during the interview. These are the types of confessions that might be of most interest to psychologists as they appear to stem directly from persuasive tactics used by an interviewer. Gudjonsson (1992) makes a distinction between *coerced-compliant* and *coerced-internalised* false confessions. *Coerced-compliant* confessions are those in which an individual confesses mainly in order to escape the aversive conditions experienced in the interview room. In such cases, the individual may know full well that they have not committed the crime, and may even realise that a confession may have serious long term consequences. Nevertheless the person feels that the pressure exerted is such that they must find some way to end the ordeal as soon as possible. If the person believes that the only way to achieve this is to sign a confession, they may take this course of action for the short-term relief that it brings.

As the name implies, *coerced-compliant confessions* are those in which the person is coerced into complying with the wishes of the interviewer even though they know that what they admit to is not true. By contrast, *coerced-internalised confessions* are those in which the suspect internalises the version of events that is being suggested by the interviewer and comes to believe that they did commit the crime in question. It is perhaps hard to imagine circumstances under which this type of confession would occur. Innocent people may have entered the interview room fairly sure that they did not commit the act of which they are suspected, and it is hard to imagine how they could be persuaded to give up this belief and accept a very different version of events. Gudjonsson and MacKeith (1982) suggest that this acceptance stems from 'memory distrust syndrome' in which the person is persuaded to question their memory of events. For example, the interviewing officer may suggest to the suspect that they cannot remember what they did because they were drunk at the time of the offence.

This type of confession is most likely to arise in circumstances where the person's original memory is perhaps rather hazy. In such a situation it may be relatively easy for the suspect to come to accept the suggestions of the interviewer, especially if it is claimed that there is 'good evidence' to support the police's version of events. However, Gudjonsson (1992) claims that it is possible for a suspect with a clear memory still to be persuaded to give up this original memory and instead to accept the version given by the police. This is most likely where the interviewer produces confusion and self doubt in the mind of the suspect.

This type of confession may be particularly problematic as the suspect may come to accept fully the version of events that has been suggested. Thus, unlike the coerced-compliant confessor, this type of individual will not try to withdraw the confession at a later date, and may plead guilty in court. We saw in Chapter 5 that when people accept misleading information they often find it hard to return to their original memory. Because suspects in these situations have accepted and internalised the version of events that has been suggested to them, they may have no reason to question whether it is actually true. If friends or family members question their guilt the person may reply by saying 'Well I confessed so that must mean that I am guilty'.

Ofshe (1989) has studied this type of confession and suggests that it is more likely to emerge when certain tactics are used by the interviewer. Specifically, the interviewer must be able to produce self-doubt and confusion in the mind of the suspect, and must be able to produce an alteration in the person's perception of reality. In order to achieve this the interrogator must convince the suspect that there is 'irrefutable' evidence against them and that there is a good and valid reason why they do not initially have a memory of having committed the crime. Ofshe suggests that there are certain specific techniques that make it more likely that this type of confession will arise. These are where the interviewer:

- repeatedly and confidently asserts a belief in the suspect's guilt

- prevents the suspect from communicating with anyone who might challenge the version of events being given by the interviewer and withholds any evidence that might support the suspect's protestations of innocence

- conducts the interview over a lengthy period of time and with great intensity

- reminds the suspect repeatedly that there is good scientific evidence that can prove their guilt

- draws attention to any memory difficulties or contradictions in what the suspect says or suggests that they are suffering from a mental disorder that has affected their memory

- insists that the suspect must accept the interviewer's version of events

- arouses fear in the suspect's mind as to what will happen if they continue to deny their involvement.

Ofshe does admit that these types of tactics are more likely to produce confessions in certain types of individuals than in others. Specifically he identifies as susceptible those people who trust authority figures, have low self confidence and are highly suggestible. Nevertheless it may be that large numbers of people may be affected to some extent by the situation in which they find themselves, simply because of the powerful situational dynamics that are found in the interview room.

Who is most likely to confess?

Gudjonsson (1991) has attempted to identify the sort of person who is most likely to be coerced into making a confession. He has developed a scale of interrogative suggestibility which he claims can separate out those more likely to confess from those who are less likely to do so. He claims that interrogative suggestibility is somewhat different from other types of suggestibility and is defined as:

> The extent to which, within a closed social interaction, people come to accept messages communicated during formal questioning as a result of which their behavioral response is affected.
>
> (Gudjonsson and Clark, 1986: 84)

Interestingly, Gudjonsson claims that his scales are applicable to witness and victim interviews in addition to interviews with suspects. The scale assesses the extent to which individuals are susceptible to leading questions and to pressure resulting from negative feedback. Typically his studies involve reading aloud a story and then asking people to recall as much detail as possible. Subjects are next asked a number of misleading questions and are then told that they have made some errors in their answers and that they will have to answer all the questions again. The 'suggestibility score' is calculated by adding together the number of questions on which people were misled the first time and the number of questions on which they shifted their answers between the first and second questioning.

Gudjonsson has found that interrogative suggestibility is correlated negatively with intelligence (i.e. those high in intelligence are generally less suggestible and those low in intelligence are generally more suggestible). However, other factors have also been found to be correlated with suggestibility, including low assertiveness, evaluative anxiety, state anxiety, and avoidance coping strategies. Adolescents under the age of 16 also appear to be more affected by negative feedback although they are not necessarily more susceptible to leading questions themselves.

Gudjonsson claims that his scales are able to differentiate between those people who resist pressure to confess and those who confess but later retract their admission. Although intelligence and memory capacity are associated with interrogative suggestibility, Gudjonsson claims that his scales can still separate out resisters from false confessors when these variables are controlled for. Gudjonsson also claims that interrogative suggestibility is linked not so much to susceptibility to leading questions themselves but rather to an inability to cope with pressure. This is reinforced by the finding that people who have previous convictions (and thus more experience of police interrogation) appear more able to resist pressure than do those appearing in the interview room for the first time.

Gudjonsson's work reinforces what may be the 'common sense' view that people low in intelligence are more likely to succumb to pressure in the interview room. However, his findings also suggest that those of normal intelligence might also be persuaded to confess if certain techniques are used. Legislation such as the Police and Criminal Evidence Act (1984) acknowledges that people of low intelligence may be vulnerable and makes provisions for such individuals to have an 'appropriate adult' present during interviews. However, Gudjonsson's work suggests that certain other types of individual may be equally vulnerable yet are not offered similar protection.

Interviewing tactics in Britain and in the US

Much of what has been said to date in this chapter is based on research carried out in the UK. The reader should be aware that since the introduction of the Police and Criminal Evidence Act (1984) many of the worst practices that police might been tempted to use have been all but eliminated. Interviews with suspects are now tape-recorded and this means that courts can decide whether the tactics used by the police during an interview were or were not fair. The Police and Criminal Evidence Act also brought in a large number of other safeguards that went some way towards protecting suspects from abuse. However, in the USA, police officers have much more freedom in the way in which they conduct interviews with suspects. Sear and Williamson (1999: 67) suggest that in the USA police officers are trained 'to use manipulative techniques with the prime objective of obtaining confessions, which are sanctioned by the judiciary'. Wakefield and Underwager (1998: 428) go even further in claiming that in the USA:

> Police freely admit deceiving suspects and lying to induce confessions. Police have fabricated evidence, made false claims about witnesses to the crimes, and falsely told suspects whatever they thought would succeed in obtaining a confession.

Such claims are somewhat disturbing, especially when coupled with the police's apparent belief that almost all suspects are guilty. Leo (1996) claims that most senior police officers and police trainers deny the possibility that the somewhat dubious manipulative tactics used could persuade an innocent person to confess. Given this situation, Leo suggests that the interviewers themselves may be completely unaware that the confession that has been obtained may be false.

The power of situations

It may be difficult for a person who has not experienced the stress of the interview room to imagine that anyone would be willing to sign a false confession simply in order to escape from the situation in which they find themselves. It may be even more difficult to imagine that an innocent person would relinquish their original memory and instead accept a version that has severe consequences for them. If we hear about an individual making a confession and then claiming that it was false, we may be unlikely to accept their retraction, preferring instead to believe that their attempt to withdraw the confession stems from a wish to avoid being punished. We may even claim that if we found ourselves in the same situation, no amount of pressure would make us admit to something that we had not done. However, such beliefs may be challenged by psychological research.

In Chapter 2 it was suggested that humans have a tendency to explain others' 'bad' behaviour by reference to internal factors, whilst explaining their own behaviour by reference to external factors. Thus if we hear of someone else making a confession we would tend to presume that it could only be because they really were guilty. In other words we would make an internal attribution when offering an explanation for the person confessing. However, this is perhaps an example of the fundamental attribution error (see Chapter 2).

Social psychology books are replete with examples of how people may succumb to situational pressures even though it may not be in their long-term interests to do so. Aronson (1999: 9) states as his first law that 'People who do crazy things are not necessarily crazy'. In Aronson's and most other social psychology texts, reference is made to a number of now infamous studies in which people have behaved in ways that appear at first glance to be almost inexplicable. In perhaps the most famous of these, volunteers were prepared to give another individual what could have been fatal electric shocks mainly because of the powerful situational forces that were in operation (Milgram, 1965). In another now infamous study (Zimbardo, 1966) students assigned to play the role of prison guards in a simulated prison quite quickly adopted sadistic and aggressive behaviour towards the 'prisoners'. The prisoners (actually fellow students) quickly became very passive and withdrawn. Partly because of concern for the welfare of the 'prisoners' this experiment had to be curtailed much sooner than had been intended.

The point about these and many other studies is that if we fail to recognise the powerful influences that situations can have on individuals we will tend to make inappropriate presumptions about individuals and their behaviours. A person who has been arrested on suspicion of having committed some crime or other will be in a relatively powerless position when interviewed. By contrast the interviewer will have a great deal of power and control over what takes place. As has been noted elsewhere:

> Being deprived of one's liberty, being made to feel that one has little control over one's immediate fate, being pressurised by an authority figure, being told that one's situation is hopeless can have a profound effect on even the most determined suspect.
>
> (Ainsworth, 1995: 48–9)

Police officers may use the power imbalance typically found in the interview room to their advantage when trying to persuade a guilty person to admit their involvement in a crime (Inbau *et al*, 1986). However, they should also be aware that in certain circumstances that power imbalance, when coupled with the use of certain tactics, may result in vulnerable individuals confessing falsely.

Summary

In this chapter we have seen some of the effects that different strategies can have on the outcome of a suspect interview. Perhaps of most interest to psychologists is the question of whether some of the techniques used by the police might persuade an innocent person to confess. Much of the research conducted to date suggests that this may, in certain circumstances occur. Research such as that conducted by Gudjonsson has identified the type of person who is most likely to be coerced into making a false confession. Psychological research has also identified a number of different types of false or coerced confession and the circumstances under which each is likely to occur. Gudjonsson (2001) has also provided a framework with which retracted confessions might be analysed.

Many of the changes introduced recently in the UK have been designed to challenge the view that all suspects are guilty and that the purpose of the interview is to elicit a confession. However, in the police service, as in many other organisations, old traditions do not die easily and it remains to be seen whether basic presumptions about suspect interviews will change over time. Results of research such as that conducted by Clarke and Milne (2001) suggest that producing change in the way in which police officers approach and conduct interviews is difficult.

In this chapter we have also seen that the detection of deception is not as straightforward as people may believe and that many police officers may have an over-inflated and unjustified belief in their ability to spot when a person is lying. The problem appears to stem from the fact that police officers often attend to inappropriate cues when trying to decide whether or not a person is lying. The research suggests that in real life there is no equivalent of Pinocchio's nose that will give a clear visual signal that a person is lying. However, the accurate detection of deception may be helped by attending to appropriate cues and, possibly by using indirect measures of detection. We have dealt only with the detection of deception in face-to-face interviews here, though the reader should be aware that psychologists are also developing techniques to assess the validity of written statements (see for example Parker and Brown, 2000; Canter and Alison, 1999).

A number of courts have already accepted expert testimony from psychologists with regard to the possibility of confessions being false. It seems likely that as knowledge increases further, such expert testimony will become more common. Police officers reading this chapter may go away with the view that psychologists are doing little more than 'causing trouble' and they may see their intervention as a potential threat to their ability to do their job. However, if psychologists are able to identify which suspects are likely to confess falsely and under what circumstances, they may prevent miscarriages of justice that not only punish the innocent but also allow the guilty to remain free.

Further reading

Canter, D. and Alison, L. (eds.) (1999) *Interviewing and Deception.* Aldershot: Ashgate.

Gudjonsson, G. H. (2002) *The Psychology of Interrogations and Confessions.* Chichester: Wiley.

Memon, A., Vrij, A. and Bull, R. (1998) *Psychology and Law: Truthfulness, Accuracy and Credibility.* Maidenhead: McGraw Hill.

Vrij, A. (2000) *Detecting Lies and Deceit: The Psychology of Lying and the Implications for Professional Practice.* Chichester: Wiley.

Chapter 8

Stress and policing

Throughout this volume we have discussed a range of duties that police officers may be called upon to perform and the way in which psychology may help in some of this work. Many people are attracted to policing because of the rich variety that the work involves. To someone stuck in a boring nine to five office job the prospect of being out and about, dealing with different incidents and different people every day, may hold considerable appeal. It is sometimes said that for a police officer no two days are ever the same and each day can offer new challenges and opportunities. Of course the down side of this rich variety of experience is that police officers need to be adaptable and be able to deal competently with a large number of different types of incident.

The variety of tasks may also lead to feelings of role ambiguity or role conflict (Tabol and Ainsworth, 2000). Role ambiguity arises when an employee receives insufficient information about their obligations and about others' expectations. Role conflict is said to arise when the expectations of different people (or groups of people) are incompatible. In addition, it should be borne in mind that, while some duties may be enjoyable and rewarding, others may be unpleasant or even dangerous. Bearing this point in mind it is perhaps unsurprising that police recruiters often list 'resilience' and 'a sense of humour' as essential qualities in the new recruit (see Chapter 3).

Research on stress has grown rapidly over the last 20 years and many different occupational groups have been studied by researchers. Some writers (e.g. Cooper *et al*, 2001) have claimed that work-related stress is a major problem in today's society and that more work days are lost through stress-related problems than from any other cause. The fact that some employees have successfully sued their employers for compensation because of stress-related illnesses has also served to concentrate the minds of many managers (Earnshaw and Cooper, 2001). In this chapter we will look at the current state of knowledge about stress and its effects and look more specifically at stress and policing.

Definitions of stress

Stress is such a commonly used word that we may well feel that we know exactly what it is and how it affects us. People often talk of being 'stressed out' or 'not being able to cope', usually because of an excess of demands placed upon them. For the police officer, a day in which the radio never seems to stop, and during which he/she is expected to rush from one job to another, may leave the officer feeling stressed and worn out by the end of the shift. Yet a very quiet day in which there is little to do and in which the shift passes extremely slowly may feel equally unpleasant for the officer. Although we may feel that we already know a lot about stress there are many findings from the research that are not so obvious and these will be reviewed in what follows.

One of the earliest and most succinct definitions of stress is that provide by Selye (1956). Selye suggests that stress can be thought of as any demand that taxes our adaptive responses. This is a simple definition yet it draws attention to the main factors that seem to be involved in stress. People encounter situations every day that require them to adapt and react. Providing that the 'demands' do not come too rapidly and that people have previous experience of dealing with these sorts of events, there will probably be little by way of a stress response. However, the person for whom the demands are coming just a little too fast or who is being asked to deal with situations of which they have little previous experience (or have not been trained adequately to deal with) is more likely to show signs of stress.

Selye's definition is helpful although inevitably not all researchers would view stress in the same way. Aronson *et al* (2002: 510) adopt a more social-psychological approach and define stress as 'The negative feelings and beliefs that arise whenever people feel unable to cope with demands from their environment'. It is interesting to see how this definition differs from that of the previous example. Selye puts the emphasis predominantly on *situations* and the demands and stress potential that each has. By contrast, the definition provided by Aronson *et al* focuses on the way in which people *react* to the demands of the environment and talks of 'feelings' and 'beliefs'. We may thus come to think of stress as referring either to things out there in the environment that lead people to become stressed or to the way in which people are affected by those environmental demands. If we take the former view, we may wish to focus upon those aspects of police work that appear to have the greatest stress potential. However, if we take the latter view we may wish to place a grater emphasis upon how officers might learn to cope with or adapt to the stressors that they encounter in their work. We will consider each of these factors in what follows.

Situations or events as stressors

It may be obvious that whilst some situations or events will have the potential to make us feel stressed, others may have the opposite effect and make us feel comfortable and relaxed. Sitting an important and very difficult examination will make most people feel anxious or 'stressed', while soaking up the sun on a golden beach will make most feel contented and relaxed. Researchers have tried to identify the sorts of situations that will tend to produce a stress response in the majority of people who encounter them.

The first systematic attempt to do this was provided by Holmes and Rahe (1967) in their Social Readjustment Rating Scale. Holmes and Rahe devised a scale of life events that many people might encounter and sought to give a 'score' to each of these. Thus at the top of the list (and given a score of 100) was 'death of spouse', closely followed by other major life events including divorce, receiving a jail term, losing one's job, death of a close family member etc. Near the bottom of the list were comparatively minor life events, including minor violations of the law, a change in work hours etc. Whilst, predictably, many of the major stressful events were those that would be viewed as unpleasant, not all fit into this category. For example, whilst being fired was given a score of 47, marriage received a score of 50 and retirement a score of 45. The reason that these 'pleasant' types of events come so high on the list is that each represents a major life change. Even changes that appear to be for the better are still changes and, as a result, may challenge our adaptive responses. As a result, events such as 'being promoted' might receive quite a high score. Essentially Holmes and Rahe suggested that the more that people are required to change and to readjust following a critical life event, the greater the stress. The loss of a close relative will, in most cases, require a great deal of readjustment, hence the high score given to such an event.

Holmes and Rahe used the scale in order to calculate a 'stress score' for individuals and to then compare this with the person's health. Thus typically Holmes and Rahe would ask people to list all the life events that they had encountered over the previous 12 months and then take a measure of the person's current level of health. The main finding was that those who had suffered the largest number of identified life events during the previous 12 months were those who reported the highest levels of ill health. By comparison, those who had encountered the fewest life events (and were thus given a low stress score) reported the lowest level of illness. The results seem to suggest two important points. Firstly, certain life events are likely to affect people in identifiable ways. Secondly, experiencing stressful events makes people more vulnerable to illness. The second point may tie in with common experience in which people may report feeling run down and then become unwell physically. Cohen *et al* (1991) suggest that even people's likelihood of catching a cold may be related to the amount of stress they are experiencing at the time that they are exposed to the cold virus.

Holmes and Rahe's work was interesting in providing evidence of how stressful certain life events can be and how they might affect people. Their findings have to some extent been confirmed by more recent work (e.g. Tesser and Beach, 1998). However, we should add some qualifications to what Holmes and Rahe claimed in their research. Firstly they appear to have suggested that each life event would have the same level of impact on each person. Clearly this view is a little too simplistic and we need to look at the circumstances that surround each life event. While the death of a spouse represents a very serious event that will affect most people deeply, some such deaths will be more distressing than others. The untimely death in a plane crash of a much-loved partner may have a catastrophic impact upon the bereaved spouse. By comparison, the eventual death of a 90 year old who has suffered a degenerative illness for many years may be seen by the surviving partner as a relief.

A second point relates to the suggestion that all people would be affected in the same way (e.g. by becoming unwell) as a result of the life events that they encounter. We must acknowledge that not all people will be affected in the same way even if the circumstances are similar. For example, for some people being promoted may be viewed as ample reward for years of hard work and the individual will relish the opportunity to demonstrate their abilities within their new role. By contrast, another individual who is promoted may have serious doubts about their ability to perform well in the their new role and will worry a great deal about how they are going to cope. As we will see later in this chapter, the way in which people perceive (or, more correctly, appraise) a change in their life will have a major impact upon them. Some see life changes as representing challenges and opportunities while others see them as threatening and view them with dread. All life events require readjustment, but for some the readjustment is more difficult than for others.

There are other criticisms of the work of Holmes and Rahe. For example, their research tended to focus on the sorts of events that might be of concern to middle class individuals. Thus things like poverty and the experience of racism were not considered, though clearly these are important and stressful aspects of life for many people. It has also been pointed out that Holmes and Rahe's work was correlational (i.e. they saw what types of life events appeared to be co-related with illness). The problem with any correlational study is that it can only demonstrate that there is a relationship between two variables, not that one *caused* the other. It may be that there is a third variable (e.g. old age) that means that certain kinds of people are more likely to be experiencing life changes and to become ill. Despite these criticisms, Holmes and Rahe's basic point (i.e. that certain life changes that require a great deal of readjustment will impact upon individuals) is still valuable.

Life events and policing

Examining life events and assessing their stress potential has helped us to understand why people react as they do to important life changes. Holmes and Rahe looked at the sort of life events that are likely to affect the majority of people, although it may also be useful to consider life events that may be peculiar to certain occupational groups. A number of studies have attempted to do this in relation to police work. Perhaps the best study of this type was that conducted by James D Sewell in the USA (Sewell, 1983). Sewell surveyed a number of police officers in the US and had them identify the sorts of work-related incidents that they found the most and the least stressful. Whilst some of the top-ranked duties may be quite predictable, others that were put near the top may not be quite so obvious. Heading the list of 144 different incidents was 'violent death of a partner in the line of duty', which was closely followed by 'dismissal' and 'taking a life or shooting someone in the line of duty'. It is easy to see why witnessing violent death, especially if it involves one's partner would be rated as particularly distressing. However, being dismissed appears to hold almost equal fear, as does the suicide of a fellow officer.

Most of the top ten ranked incidents involve violence, threat, or danger but not far behind these are a range of other types of events that were ranked highly. For example, 'being passed over for promotion' is given the same score as 'pursuit of an armed suspect'. Equally interesting is that 'observing an act of police corruption' is ranked slightly higher than having to deal with a hostage situation or with a barricaded suspect. There are other rankings that, at least in the non-police reader, may evoke some surprise. For example, being investigated by the internal affairs department is ranked five points above having to try to control a riot.

What is clear from research of this kind is that there are stressors within the job of policing that might not be so obvious to an outsider. If questioned about police work, most outside observers would tend to list the dangerous aspects of the job as being those that pose the greatest threat in terms of stress. However, as with most other jobs, there are a large number of organisational and management stressors that can have as much of an impact as facing physical danger. For example, seeing a less experienced or less competent colleague being promoted above us would be disturbing to most workers, and was ranked 22nd (out of 144) by the police officers in Sewell's sample. Most people might also agree about the stress involved in failing an exam that would qualify us for promotion (ranked 34th by the officers).

Recent research has sought to establish why certain types of incident are seen as particularly stressful. As was noted above, those that involve physical danger or threat are understandably ranked quite highly. However, there are other types of incident that could not be classed in this way that can nevertheless affect people significantly. Although we talked earlier about 'threat' in the physical sense, there can be other forms of 'threat' that can lead to difficulties. For example, some incident that represents a threat to our self esteem or feeling of competency may be seen as potentially harmful. Thus having a complaint made against one or being the subject of an internal investigation will be seen as psychologically (as opposed to physically) threatening.

There are a number of other sorts of situations that typically evoke a stress response. These are those that involve *conflict* and those that involve a *loss of control*.

Conflicting demands

Here the term conflict is used not to indicate aggression and argument but more a conflict between competing demands. If for example we know that we should stay in and study this evening but have just been invited out to a party, we will tend to experience a conflict, whatever we eventually decide to do. In this case, the two sets of 'demands' are in conflict with each other and as a result there is no easy way to resolve the dilemma. It has been suggested that police officers often find themselves in this type of conflict situation as there are so many competing demands placed upon them. For example, pressure from a senior officer to report more motorists for minor traffic offences may conflict with the community constable's wish to establish a good rapport with the community in general. Police officers of all ranks often find themselves struggling to cope with the large number of conflicting demands that are placed upon them. Each section of a community (not to mention each political party) may have different views as to the priorities that the police should establish. All this will need to be balanced with demands from central and local government, many of which may appear to be in opposition to each other.

There are other forms that 'conflict' might take. For example, in the Sewell survey discussed above, 'observing an act of police corruption', 'accepting a bribe' and 'participating in an act of police corruption' all came in the top 20 critical life events identified by police officers. These situations appear to represent conflict (or a moral dilemma) for police officers. The individual may be torn, knowing that the act of corruption is 'wrong' and that it should be reported. However, the officer may also be conscious of the solidarity within police ranks, whose rule is that you should never inform on a colleague.

Control

If you think back to Selye's definition of stress discussed earlier, it was said that stress can be anything that taxes or challenges our adaptive resources. Most of the time we may feel that we are 'in control' but sometimes the demands build up to the point where we know we are 'losing it'. In this case the 'it' that we are losing is probably the feeling of control. Most people feel that they have some degree of control over things that happen to them. For example, we may feel that as long as we drive within the speed limits and drive carefully we are unlikely to be involved in an accident. Police officers may also believe that if they do everything 'by the book' they are unlikely to have a complaint made against them. However, in some cases this feeling of control is somewhat illusory and in reality people can sometimes do little to prevent unpleasant things happening to them.

Although there has recently been a shift of emphasis in policing (e.g. towards 'policing by objectives') much of police work remains *reactive* in the sense that the police have to react or respond to demands made upon them by members of the public. To a large extent the police have little control over the rate at which these demands come in and the expectations that the public have in terms of a police response. The distraught old lady who reports an aggravated burglary in progress at her home would hardly expect to be told by the police officer taking the call 'We're a bit busy at the moment love, so ring back later'. Perhaps the best that a harried police force can hope to do is to prioritise demands for their services and respond to the most serious and pressing calls. The problem for the public, however, is that in their view each and every call to the police is important and should be responded to immediately.

Policing will always be a job where control is never fully achievable because demands upon a police force fluctuate and are never entirely predictable. The local chief superintendent may know how many officers are needed to keep the peace on an 'average' Saturday night but may be unable to say how many will be needed on any one particular Saturday evening. Thus the officers on duty on an exceptionally troublesome Saturday evening may be unable to control the number of calls demanding their attention and will feel stressed.

Individual differences and the experience of stress

So far it has been suggested that there are a number of types of situation that have the capacity to evoke a stress response. However, in many of these situations it is not possible to predict with a high degree of certainty whether a stress response will follow. The reason for this is that different people respond to stressful events in different ways. Even if we examine some of the most serious life events identified in the Holmes and Rahe study, it does seem that some people are able to cope better than others. Police officers will undoubtedly have come across some victims of quite serious crime who appear largely unaffected by their ordeal, whereas others go to pieces following a much more trivial incident. It also appears that some police officers are better able to cope with the demanding nature of their role while others succumb easily to relatively trivial daily hassles. One officer may show signs of cracking as the demands increase, while another may positively thrive on the pressure and relish the opportunity to perform well even when time is short.

There are a number of variables that appear to explain why some people respond positively to stressful situations while others buckle under the strain. We will look at some of these in the next section. Before considering these, however, we must bear in mind that an individual's appraisal of a stressor is largely a subjective process. Some people view as threatening some situations that others would find exciting and enjoyable – scary fun fair rides provide one example. People's appraisal may also be based on what they think they can do, rather than what they can do. Thus although a person might say 'I'd die if I had to do x' the chances are that if they had to do x they would not actually die.

Feelings of control

Earlier we made the point that some situations are felt to be aversive because we do not have control over what happens. However, individuals vary in their beliefs about how much control they actually have over events in their life. Rotter (1966) devised a scale that assessed the extent to which people feel that they do or do not have control over events in their life. It was found that some people score highly in terms of their tendency to believe that they have control over their own destiny whilst others scored much lower and believed that fate or luck played a large part in their lives.

Perceived control can be important. For example, it appears that people who believe that they have some control over what happens to them are more likely to fight against things that affect them. By contrast, those at the other extreme may simply 'give up'. Thus some cancer patients may do everything that they can to fight their illness while others will simply give up and accept their fate (Folkman and Moscowitz, 2000). Those who feel that they have control over their fate are much more likely to report better mental and physical health than are those who express a more fatalistic attitude. However, in some cases a feeling of loss of control can have a significant effect on an individual and add to feelings of stress.

Perhaps paradoxically, those who feel that they have a great deal of control over their fate are the ones most likely to be affected by a sudden loss of control. By contrast, those who believe that they have never had much control over what happens to them may be relatively unfazed by the same incident and add it to the long list of bad things that they have been unable to do anything about. A male police officer of the latter type who is shot and injured while on duty may simply feel that he was unlucky and wait for the injury to heal. However, an officer who has always believed that he was able to stay safe by being careful and vigilant may have a harder time adjusting to his new status as a victim. He will need to readjust his view of the world in order to come to terms with the fact that there are some things in life that we just cannot control. Unlike the fatalistic officer described earlier, this officer may not simply accept what happened to him and may try even harder to exert control in the future.

We generally talk in negative terms about a person who tries hard to exert complete control over their environment, using terms such as 'control freak' to describe someone at the extreme end of this tendency. Yet we may also make derogatory remarks about someone at the opposite extreme of the scale who simply accepts their lot in life and makes no attempt to 'take control of their life'. An interesting recent innovation in the western world is the appearance of 'life coaches' whose main purpose appears to be to help individuals to decide what they really want to do (or who they want to be) and help them to achieve these goals by taking more control. The only danger in this is that the person may feel a failure if they do not achieve their goals, despite having taken great strides to bring about the desired changes.

A police officer who wishes to achieve promotion may do all that he/she can in order to achieve this goal. If all these personal efforts prove to be in vain and the officer does not achieve his/her ambition there may be a great feeling of frustration and disappointment. However, there may be a difference in the way in which different officers respond to this disappointment and in particular the way in which they explain their 'failure' to others and to themselves. The officer may for example explain it as being just 'bad luck'. Alternatively the officer may try to blame others in the organisation (e.g. their immediate supervisor) for their lack of success. The officer may even accept responsibility and admit that they really didn't deserve the promotion, at least at this stage of their career. The point is that the exact same event will be explained and reacted to differently, depending on a number of factors within the individual. As such it is inappropriate to view stress as simply something that is 'out there' in the environment that will affect most people in the same way.

Personality 'types'

We can perhaps accept that different people will react to challenges and stressors in their lives differently. Some researchers have suggested that there are two distinct personality types with very different ways of dealing with stressors. These have been characterised as *Type A* and *Type B*.

Type A personalities are very competitive, impatient, hostile, aggressive and very much control-oriented. By comparison, Type Bs are patient, relaxed and generally non-competitive and are much more likely to 'go with the flow'. Most people will be able to identify some friends or acquaintances who fit neatly into one of these categories (although some individuals appear to be somewhere in between). Although they may not be very popular, Type As tend to be the ruthless go-getters who get where they want to go and don't care too much about who they trample on along the way. However, achieving one ambition will tend not to satisfy such a person and they will head off in search of some new challenge rather than be satisfied with what they have achieved.

Although Type As are likely to be more successful in their careers, they will not necessarily feel any happier about what they have achieved. Such individuals are likely to become workaholics, so fundamental is their need to prove themselves and to 'succeed'. However, this type of individual is significantly more likely to suffer coronary heart disease than is the Type B individual. Recent research (e.g. Farber and Burge-Callaway, 1998) has attempted to narrow down which aspects of the Type A personality are the most dangerous in terms of vulnerability to stress-related illness. It appears that competitiveness and a fast pace of life may not in themselves make people more vulnerable, but that if they are accompanied by a great deal of hostility within the individual then there are clear dangers.

Gender, race and stress

Before leaving our discussion of individual factors that might affect police officers' ability to deal with stress, we should perhaps consider whether the race and gender of the officer might be relevant. This is not to suggest that female or ethnic minority officers are less able to cope on a personal level, but rather that certain features of the police organisation might make it more likely that such officers may experience additional problems.

It has been noted at various points in this book that policing remains a job that is carried out largely by males. As a result, females are not only in the minority numerically, but are also in the minority in terms of the establishment of occupational norms (Brown, 2000b). As with many male-dominated occupations, there is within the police service an emphasis on toughness and controlling emotions. An individual who is unable to demonstrate these qualities may be perceived as weak or unsuited to the job of policing. The prejudiced views of some male officers mean that women within the police service may well be regarded in this way, thus adding to any other stressors inherent within the work. Westmorland (2001: 175) also notes that male structures and belief systems are so pervasive in the police that women officers rarely feel valued or accepted.

Within police organisations, there is a heavy emphasis on solidarity and mutual support. Such solidarity and mutual support is vital in the dangerous and unpredictable world of policing. However, as Brown (2000b: 260) notes:

This may work powerfully in favour of those who belong to the majority social categories of white male. However, for those who are different, or 'other', such as from ethnic minorities or women, the informal culture places additional burdens on officers and excludes them from the informal support systems.

Female officers may thus suffer the indignity and stress of working within a prejudiced organisation, yet cannot call upon the same peer support or coping mechanisms available to male officers.

Reactions to stress

When people report experiencing stress, they often complain of a range of physical symptoms. These can range from indigestion to stomach ulcers and from tiredness to severe depression. The reason why these symptoms are produced is that the human body reacts physically to the experience of stress. Throughout our evolution, humans have survived by reacting to danger in certain ways. When faced with a threat, humans' bodies tend to respond by altering the levels of a number of important bodily chemicals (e.g. adrenaline). This has been referred to as the *fight or flight response*. This term refers to the fact that, when faced with a threat, our body prepares us to be able to stand and fight off the threat or to run away from the danger. When humans led a more primitive and dangerous life than is the case today, this reaction was essential to survival. However, whilst the threats and dangers from predators may have receded, our bodies still react to any potentially dangerous or stressful situation in the same way. Thus a police officer who has to deal with a potentially dangerous situation may experience the same sorts of physiological arousal as did an ancestor facing a wild animal.

These days humans may well perceive 'threat' differently than in the past. Thus if we have to give a talk in front of a large audience for the first time, or are required to give evidence in an intimidating courtroom, our bodies may 'prepare' us for this ordeal by secreting the appropriate chemicals and readying us to be able to fight or run away. The problem is that if we experience these reactions too frequently our physical health can suffer. For some people, recognition of what is happening to them will lead to help being sought. However, other people may choose to ignore the early warning signs of stress and carry on until such time as their bodies or minds cry 'enough' and some kind of breakdown occurs. As the cynic might remark 'Death is nature's way of telling you to slow down'.

Recognising and admitting that one is suffering from stress may be easier for some people than for others. Some organisations also make it relatively easy for employees to seek and receive appropriate help, while others are reluctant to admit that there may be a problem and will expect those who cannot cope to simply leave (Earnshaw and Cooper, 2001). In an organisation such as the police service, admitting that one is suffering in this way can be a problem. The predominantly male culture of policing has traditionally engendered an atmosphere in which to admit that one is suffering from stress is tantamount to admitting that one is weak and cannot do the job. Supervisors and colleagues may be unsympathetic and fall back upon hackneyed expression such as 'If you can't stand the heat, get out of the kitchen'.

Police officers may cover up their true feelings, especially when with colleagues. As a consequence, police officers may, at least on the surface, laugh off many incidents that would have ordinary members of the public reaching for the tranquillisers. Police officers may appear to be callous and unfeeling, though in some cases this facade can hide underlying feelings of concern. More recently this 'tough' attitude has been challenged and many police forces now recognise the potential for any employee to suffer from stress.

As we saw above, there are a number of reasons why policing might be considered a potentially stressful occupation. Not only might there be daily encounters with threatening people and dangerous situations, but other organisational factors might add to the strain of doing a difficult and demanding job. Blau (1994) makes a distinction between external and internal stressors. Included in the former are things such as the court system, the media, community attitudes etc., while in the latter are factors such as poor training, poor career opportunities, inadequate rewards and excessive paperwork The diverse sources of police stress are also considered by Toch (2002), who suggests that, at least in the US, departmental politics and top-down management practices are perhaps more stress-inducing than the dangers on the street. This same author also draws attention to the current importance of race and gender issues. Biggam *et al* (1997) suggest that such issues are also relevant to police officers in Scotland.

Blau suggests that recognition of the diverse sources of stress is important. He states that many police officers find themselves in a very difficult position with 'great expectations from the community, rigid demands from management, relatively little support, and limited appreciation' (Blau, 1994: 188).

In many cases, the stresses and strains of policing will build up slowly and it may be some time before any individual shows signs of being affected. However, in policing there is always the potential for some cataclysmic event to occur which almost single-handedly can affect the most resilient officer. We will next consider one possible consequence of this.

Post-traumatic stress disorder (PTSD)

As the name implies, post-traumatic stress disorder refers to stress reactions that can occur following the experience of a particularly unpleasant life event. It is now recognised that some battle-scarred soldiers who broke down and were perhaps punished for not obeying orders in wartime may have been suffering from this syndrome. Members of the emergency services who have had to deal with distressing incidents (e.g. fires, transportation accidents or the deaths of children) may experience many of the symptoms associated with this condition. Victims of crime may also report PTSD symptoms for several weeks after their victimisation (Ainsworth, 2000: 36). In cases such as rape, victims may report severe symptoms months or even years after they have been attacked (Shipherd and Beck, 1999). The most common symptoms are nightmares, sleep disturbances, flashbacks and general or specific anxiety.

For police officers, PTSD may be experienced as a result of dealing with the aftermath of major incidents or as a result of incidents in which they have been involved personally. Seeing a partner killed, narrowly escaping death themselves, or having to shoot a suspect, are all the kinds of incidents that may give rise to PTSD. Many police forces now recognise the potential consequences of experiencing these sorts of incidents and insist that officers speak to a counsellor/psychologist in the immediate aftermath of such an experience. It is also not uncommon for forces to set up critical incident debriefing sessions in which all those involved in major incident have an opportunity to discuss the incident and their reactions.

Bohl (1995) notes that it was not until relatively recently that many police organisations recognised that officers might experience the sorts of symptoms characteristic of PTSD. This belated recognition was explained by reference to two factors. Firstly, it was thought that because police officers deal with emergency situations on an almost daily basis, they are less likely to succumb than would a person unused to this type of incident. The second assumption was that if PTSD symptoms did occur, they did so in a very small percentage of officers, and so no special measures need be taken.

Both of these assumptions have been challenged in recent years and it is now recognised that significant numbers of officers can be affected. Furthermore it is also acknowledged that, if left untreated, the symptoms can have long lasting effects both on the officer and, indirectly, on the organisation itself. It should, however, be noted that making help available to officers does not guarantee that they will use it. As noted earlier, if there is a macho, tough ethos within the organisation, it will be difficult for officers to admit to their colleagues that they do wish to seek help. Officers may also feel that if they admit to such problems their chances of promotion may be affected. For this reason, more enlightened police forces generally make counselling available on a confidential basis and, at least in theory, allow consultations to be held without an officer's colleagues or superiors being aware of this.

A great deal more is known about PTSD today than was the case only a few years ago. While we know the sorts of incidents that may be most likely to elicit symptoms, it is still not easy to predict who will and who will not experience problems. Some recent research (Wellbrook, 1999) suggests that female officers may be more likely to experience PTSD symptoms than male officers although this may be partly accounted for by the fact that female officers reported feeling less accepted within the police organisation. Some other interesting recent work (Anshel, 2000) has looked at the coping styles of different officers and suggested ways in which coping mechanisms can be improved.

Critical incident debriefing and stress counselling

Bohl (1995) has developed a quite sophisticated programme of critical incident debriefing based on crisis theory. He advocates the widespread adoption of this sort of technique, arguing that in his approach:

> Treatment is brief, immediate and directed toward alleviation of present symptoms, prevention of future symptoms, and restoration of an earlier level of functioning.
>
> (Bohl, 1995: 185)

The technique is thus more suited to officers who have experienced one particularly harrowing incident than to the officer who has allowed stress levels to build up over a long period of time and is now showing signs of stress or burn-out. For the latter type of case, a slightly different approach may be more appropriate (Blau, 1994: Chapter 8; Alexander, 1999). We should, however, be aware that officers who appear to need, but do not, receive help may try to deal with their discomfort and distress in a maladaptive way. Officers may, for example, consume excessive amounts of alcohol as a way of helping them to relax or to cope with their feelings (Richmond *et al*, 1999). In some police organisations, drinking is seen as an almost integral part of the 'role' of police officer and those who do not join in are treated with derision. It may also be the case that job-related stress can lead to significant increases in the level of cynicism expressed by serving officers (Thomas-Riddle, 2000).

We should acknowledge finally that some types of police work appear to be more stressful than others. For example, officers working on undercover assignments often report greater stress symptoms than do patrol officers (Farkas, 1986). Assignments to areas with particularly bad reputations may also lead to heightened vulnerability to stress-related symptoms, and any counselling service must recognise these differences. We should also mention the fact that, whilst most research has looked at the stress experienced by police officers who are junior in rank, there is some evidence to suggest that more senior officers may suffer similar levels of stress. For example, Brown *et al* (1996) found that officers in middle or senior management positions reported high levels of stress, much of which revolved around organisational structure, co-worker relations and their managerial role.

Summary

We have seen in this chapter that there are a number of different ways of conceptualising stress. Stress can refer both to difficult events in the environment and to the unpleasant feelings generated within the individual. Whilst it is true that there are a large number of different 'life stressors', people also vary widely in the way in which they deal with potentially stressful life events.

We have also seen that there are a number of reasons why an understanding of stress is important within the police organisation. A build up of stress within individual officers can have a detrimental effect on both the officers themselves and on the police organisation that they serve. Officers who find it difficult to deal with the stresses involved in police work may be helped through appropriate psychological counselling. However, it should also be acknowledged that a large number of officers might be affected by particular events, and for them critical incident debriefing may be invaluable in reducing the likelihood of developing PTSD.

Our understanding of stress had advanced enormously over recent years. A clear understanding of both the general principles of stress and the specific problems faced by police officers will help both police officers and police organisations to function more effectively. Organisations that ignore the potential problems that stress can cause for police officers are likely to encounter significant problems (Parent and Verdun-Jones, 2000)

Further reading

Cooper, C. L. (2000) *Conquer Your Stress*. London: CIPD.

Cooper, C. L., Dewe, P. J. and Driscoll, M. P. (2001) *Organisational Stress: A Review and Critique of Theory, Research & Applications*. London: Sage.

Toch, H. (2002) *Stress in Policing*. Washington DC: American Psychological Association.

Violanti, J. M. and Paton, D. (eds.) (1999) *Police Trauma: Psychological Aftermath of Civilian Combat*. Springfield IL: Charles C Thomas.

Chapter 9

Crime patterns and offender profiling

One of the police's main roles is the prevention and detection of crime. In order to demonstrate their effectiveness in these tasks it will be necessary to provide an accurate record of the number of crimes that occur in any given area each year. A great deal of police work involves the recording of crime information and the compilation of annual statistics. Once recorded, comparisons can then be made between crime rates in different regions or changes in the crime rate over time. However, the accumulation of such data can also be of benefit to a police force in allowing crime analysts to identify any trends in the pattern of crime. Analysts can, for example, identify crime 'hot spots' and, as a result, allow resources to be deployed more effectively. Analysis of crime data also allows crime reduction initiatives to be evaluated.

In recent years there has been increased interest in the area of crime analysis and crime pattern analysis. This has been helped by the ready availability of personal computers that can be used to analyse large amounts of data. For example, the availability of geographic information systems allows the police to see at a glance where and when different types of crime are occurring in their area. When information about known offenders is added to the system, it becomes easier to identify the sorts of individuals who are likely to be involved. Systematic analysis of crime data and crime patterns allows the police to be more effective in the fight against crime and this is becoming recognised increasingly today. In this chapter we will look at crime trends and patterns and also examine the way in which the profiling of offenders may be useful.

The distribution of offending

Crime statistics can provide valuable information about crime levels within a given area but may not in themselves be particularly useful in helping the police to target their resources effectively. For example, knowing that there were 1000 burglaries in a particular area of Manchester last year tells us that there is a burglary problem, but little else. In order to be useful, the data will need to be broken down and examined more carefully. We may for example find that most burglaries are confined to a small area or that they tend to be committed at certain times of the day, or on certain days of the week. Further analysis may reveal that there are similarities between the methods used in some of the burglaries, perhaps suggesting that the same offender is likely to be involved.

It is only in recent years that the police have begun to see the potential of crime analysis and have employed specialists to take on this role. To some extent they have been helped by psychologists, who have been able to offer valuable insights into why crime occurs in the way that it does. Psychologists bring with them a scientific approach and an emphasis on the objective analysis of data. It is through such methods that progress is most likely. Perhaps the best way of illustrating this is to consider why and how some crimes occur.

The first point to make is that crime is not distributed randomly. A basic analysis of recorded crime in any given area will tend to reveal clusters or pockets of activity. In some cases, the reason for such clusters is blindingly obvious. For example, car crime is more likely to occur in areas where there is a high density of cars, and personal assaults more likely in areas where there are a large number of bars and young people congregate. Any analysis must thus start with an examination of the types of crime occurring and the areas in which they are to be found. However, going beyond this basic analysis will be much more helpful in discerning something about offences and offenders. For example, we may notice that one housing estate has a large number of burglaries whilst one nearby has a much lower rate. Further analysis might help to identify the most probable reason for this discrepancy.

It may seem an obvious point but we need to bear in mind the fact that offences are most likely in areas where offenders are to be found (Anselin *et al*, 1999). Earlier we made the point that assaults are perhaps more likely in areas where young people congregate, especially if alcohol is widely available. The areas around bars and clubs will tend to become hot spots of crime, the reason for which will become obvious especially if one considers the timing of the offences. However, it may also be the case that violence is more likely around certain bars and clubs than others.

Further analysis would need to try to establish why this is the case. It may for example be that one club attracts more violent people than another, partly because of the reputation that the place has established. Alternatively, it may be that one bar has little in the way of security and, as a result, those contemplating violence will be undeterred.

The point to emphasise here is that there may well be a large number of reasons why a particular crime (or series of crimes) occurred. We may be tempted to jump to simplistic conclusions when asked to provide an explanation for a particular criminal act. However, it will rarely be possible to identify one single causative factor that will explain fully why a particular offence occurred. This does not, however, prevent people (including some police officers) from jumping to simplistic conclusions and suggesting simplistic remedies.

An interesting perspective on crime occurrences is offered by routine activity theory (Cohen and Felson, 1979). According to this theory, for a crime to occur there must be three elements: a motivated offender, a suitable victim and the absence of a 'capable guardian'. This may appear to be an obvious point yet it helps to explain why crime levels are as high as they are, especially in big cities. According to the theory, the modern city readily brings together the three elements that are necessary for a crime to be committed. Thus every city will have within it a number of suitably motivated offenders. It will also contain a large number of vulnerable victims or targets. In many cases there will also be no 'capable guardian' who might otherwise deter the offender who is contemplating committing a crime. Cohen and Felson's work has encouraged criminologists and psychologists to move beyond the simplistic analysis of the offender and their motivations. More recent work that considers target or victim selection and situational crime prevention initiatives focus more upon the second and third of Cohen and Felson's elements. We will say more about these later in this chapter.

Accounting for criminal events

One thing that psychologists try to do is to consider all the factors that are relevant when trying to understand and explain any piece of behaviour. Thus psychologists may today take into account genetic factors and the influence of personality, in addition to considering the many situational and environmental influences that may be likely to affect behaviour. Many early writers tended to focus on one particular aspect when trying to explain criminal behaviour. For example, Eysenck (1964) believed that personality may exert a strong influence on the individual. He suggested that people with certain personality characteristics were much more likely to offend than were people with different personality traits. Eysenck believed that personality was largely genetically determined and as a result he argued that genetics play a significant part in explaining criminal behaviour.

Few criminologists and psychologists today would try to explain criminal behaviour in such simplistic terms. Even if it were to be proved that people with a certain type of personality or a certain genetic make-up were more likely to offend, we would still need to consider when, where and how the person chose to commit their illegal acts. It is this recognition that has prompted psychologists to look more closely at victim selection and situational elements in offending behaviour.

Crime analysis and the choice of victims

Many people fear victimisation and will do whatever they can to prevent becoming a victim themselves. However, recent research that has focused upon victim or target selection suggests that whether or not one becomes a victim is hardly a matter of chance. One often-quoted figure produced by Farrell and Pease (1993) is that 4% of the population suffer 44% of recorded crime. It would be naïve to think that this 4% are simply unfortunate – in many cases the reason why they have been targeted may be obvious. For example, an off-licence with little or no security in a run down area of town might make an ideal target for those who wish to obtain alcohol, cigarettes or money. By contrast the up-market wine shop with state of the art CCTV in a well-protected shopping precinct may be less likely to be targeted.

Any analysis of crime patterns must take into account the characteristics of the victim or target chosen and the situational factors that surround the offence. Such consideration will allow one to go beyond the picture that might be provided by a few coloured pins stuck in a map. Although, as noted above, the reason for the selection of a particular target or victim may be immediately obvious, some of the factors that appear relevant may not be quite so predictable.

One obvious factor in victimisation is residential location. Most people will know whether the area in which they live or work has a reputation as a high or a low crime area. Insurance companies may also be aware of this and will charge much higher premiums for those unfortunate enough to live in the area regarded as high risk. However, information contained within the British Crime Survey (Mirrlees-Black *et al*, 1998) has identified a number of different variables associated with location. Along with obvious risk factors (e.g. living in an inner city area or on a council estate) were some that might not be quite so apparent (e.g. living on a main or through road, and living in the North of England).

When one looks specifically at burglary there are again some fairly obvious risk factors and some that might not be quite so apparent to the casual observer. For example, we might expect factors such as the type of property, and whether or not it is left unoccupied for long periods of time, to be relevant risk factors. However, not so immediately obvious would be variables such as the age of the head of the household, whether it is a single parent household, and whether the head of the household was unemployed or on a low income. Any analysis of crime trends and patterns must take into account the sort of persons or properties that are targeted and the reasons behind such targeting. Only then might we begin to understand, explain and perhaps prevent further victimisation.

We must bear in mind that any attempt to analyse crime patterns and trends is reliant upon accurate data being available in the first place. Crime analysts can only work with the information that they have been given, and in many cases this will not tell the whole story. There are a whole series of stages that need to be negotiated before a crime appears within the official statistics (Ainsworth, 2001: Chapter 4). By no means all crimes will be reported, and even if they are, not all will be recorded by the police. (The British Crime Survey suggests that less than half of some types of crime are reported to the police.) Of those that are reported and recorded, some may not be recorded accurately. For example, the police may record an attempted burglary as criminal damage to a front door, or may record the location of the offence inaccurately. These points should be born in mind in the sections that follow.

Repeat victimisation

For many people becoming a victim of crime may be traumatic and some will struggle to come to terms with their situation. However, for a number of people, becoming a victim once is not the end of the matter. As we will see in what follows, people or properties that are victimised once have a significantly heightened risk of being targeted in the future. One of the most prolific and valuable areas of research over recent years has been the study of repeat victimisation. The concept refers to persons or properties that are targeted more than once over a set period of time.

When one learns about what the research has shown it may appear to be 'obvious' yet it has fallen on psychologists such as Ken Pease (1998) to demonstrate the regularity with which repeat victimisation occurs. Pease has gone so far as to suggest that the best single predictor of future victimisation is past victimisation. Having identified how widespread repeat victimisation is, it is then possible for the police to use this information to their advantage. They can, for example, channel crime prevention efforts towards recently victimised targets, in the knowledge that they are likely to be targeted again in the near future.

As with other victimisation, it is sometimes fairly obvious why a repeat has occurred. For example, a child who continues to live with a violent and abusive father may suffer repeated attacks until either the child or the father is removed. A man who makes a habit of getting drunk and then insulting all those around him may also become a regular victim of assaults. However, in other cases, the reason for repeat victimisation may prove to be somewhat more elusive. For example, 'common sense' might suggest that burglars would make a point of targeting a new property each time they went out. This appears, however, not to be the case.

As we saw above, not all people and properties are equally vulnerable to crime. Many of the 4% of the population that experience 44% of the crime referred to above will have been victimised more than once. In some cases their repeat victimisation will be offence specific (i.e. they will have suffered a repeat offence of a similar type to the original), whereas in other cases the subsequent victimisation may involve a different type of crime. The latter type of repeat may perhaps be put down to the area in which the person lives – in a particularly high crime area, a person may have both their house broken into and their car stolen. However, repeats that are offence-specific may demand somewhat closer examination.

Pease (1996) suggests that there are perhaps two explanations as to why a repeat occurs in cases such as burglary. The first of these he refers to as the *flag* hypothesis – certain features of the house flag it up as an easy or desirable target. According to this view, a house is selected again because it suffers from an enduring level of risk. The reasons that it was selected as a target in the first place are still there and, as a result, it is likely to be selected as a target again (providing that the factors that made it an attractive target in the first place have not been changed).

The second possible explanation is referred to as the *boost* hypothesis. According to this viewpoint, committing a first offence against a certain property 'boosts' the chances that it will be selected again in the future. It may be, for example, that a burglar tells a fellow offender of the rich pickings that are to be found at a certain house that he has recently burgled. Armed with this information, the other offender may target the same property rather than selecting another home at random. Alternatively, the first offender may decide to target the same property again in the future. He may, for example, have noticed that there are valuable antiques in the house and he will need to return later with a large van in order to remove the larger items. Alternatively the burglar may be aware that items that were stolen on the first visit will have been replaced after a few weeks and that if he breaks in again he is likely to find a haul of newer and perhaps more valuable items to steal.

People generally feel more comfortable in environments with which they are familiar. This also appears to apply to criminals such as burglars. When first selecting a target a burglar may see two types of houses, i.e. those that appear to make suitable targets and those that do not (Bennett, 1995). However, if the burglar is walking down the street in which he has committed previous offences, he will now see three types of houses, i.e. those that do not make suitable targets, those that do, and those with which he is already familiar (which by definition will have previously been labelled 'suitable'). In these circumstances it is perhaps unsurprising that the burglar will be drawn towards the property of which he already has some knowledge. He may know his way around the house and know that there are unlikely to be any nasty surprises (e.g. a large dog in the kitchen). He may also reason that, as his activities were unseen by neighbours last time, he is unlikely to be spotted on this occasion.

Pease suggests that committing the first offence educates the burglar and, as a result, makes it more likely that they will return to the same property in the future. This reasoning falls within the explanations for offending that are offered by *rational choice theory*. This theory suggests that when criminals are deciding where and when to commit an offence, they will weigh up the risks and potential benefits and make a 'rational choice' as to the most suitable target. Research in which burglars have been asked about their selection of targets (e.g. Bennett and Wright, 1984) offers some support for this notion. Burglars do appear to consider whether the anticipated rewards associated with a particular target outweigh the risks. In the case of repeats, burglars have a better indication of the level of risk involved and better knowledge of the likely rewards. Bearing this in mind, we can see why burglars may be more likely to choose the previously victimised property rather than one that is unknown to them.

Pease's work has proved extremely useful for the police. He has been able to demonstrate the likelihood of repeat victimisation and, as a result, allow the police to target their limited resources more effectively. If the police have some knowledge of where and when offences are likely to take place in the future, they will be in a much better position to be able either to prevent these offences or be ready and waiting when the offender returns. There are other useful aspects of Pease's work. For example, he has discovered that if repeats do occur they are likely to be in the first few weeks after the original offence. The longer the time period following the first attack, the less likely it is that a second offence will occur. Bearing this in mind, there would be some value in offering additional protection to the targeted household in the immediate aftermath of the first attack but little justification for maintaining this for months after the original offence.

Policing has often been seen as reactive – the police wait for a call for their services and then respond appropriately. However, in recent years, policing has tried to move towards a more proactive stance in which patrolling becomes more targeted and initiatives are introduced that will reduce crime. Knowledge accumulated by the analysis of crime patterns and trends makes the introduction of such initiatives easier. Furthermore knowledge of factors such as the likelihood of repeat victimisation allows a much more focused approach to crime reduction to be taken. The study of repeat victimisation provides perhaps one of the best examples of the way in which psychology and policing can be brought together profitably. In the rest of this chapter we will look at some other areas in which psychology may be of value to those working in the policing area.

The relevance of place and target selection

In the early part of this chapter we made the point that in order to understand why crime events occur it is necessary to consider all the relevant variables. Recently attention has shifted away from the study of offenders themselves and moved towards a greater consideration of the environmental aspects that may be associated with offending. Some of these were touched upon earlier but a more detailed consideration may be appropriate at this stage.

Perhaps the starting point for this focus can be seen as the development of situational crime prevention measures (Clarke, 1983). As its title implies, situational crime prevention is concerned primarily with the offence itself and not so much with the offender. The approach presumes that a great deal of crime is opportunistic – thus reducing opportunities will reduce crime levels (Mayhew *et al*, 1976). As such there is an emphasis on practical measures that might discourage criminal activity. In some cases this might involve modifications to the physical environment in order that crime might be curtailed.

Clarke (1992) suggests that crime might be prevented or discouraged in one of three ways:

1. Increasing the amount of effort involved in committing a crime.

2. Increasing the perceived level of risk involved in committing an offence.

3. Reducing the likely rewards of criminal activity.

In some cases crime reduction initiatives have attempted to incorporate all three of these steps, although other more specific initiatives have targeted just one or possibly two. A detailed consideration of situational crime prevention is beyond the scope of this text, but the reader may wish to consider the presumptions that are inherent within the approach. The theory suggests that all but the most determined of criminals may be discouraged from committing crime if we increase the 'costs' of offending (i.e. effort and risk) and decrease the likely rewards. Studies that have interviewed offenders (e.g. Bennett and Wright, 1984) offer some support for this viewpoint. This knowledge provides us with a better understanding of why certain patterns in criminal activity occur, and allows us to introduce measures that might prevent further offending.

Geographic profiling

In addition to understanding why certain crimes occur at certain locations, detailed knowledge of patterns of offending allows us to gain more insights into the offender and, in particular, their likely place of residence (Canter and Larkin, 1993; Davies and Dale, 1995; Rossmo, 1997). Much of the work on geographic profiling examines the relationship between clusters of offences and the offender. Research that has examined offenders' choice of offence locations suggests that most offenders display fairly predictable patterns. Burglars, for example, rarely select houses in a random or haphazard way, but rather tend to choose targets within certain well-defined boundaries. In most cases, the locations of their offences will be related to their home base (Wiles and Costello, 2000).

Armed with this knowledge, it becomes possible to hypothesise about an offender's most likely place of residence. Several researchers have suggested that if one is able to draw a circle that encompasses all the crimes committed by an offender, there is a high probability that the offender will live within that circle. Some studies have attempted to go even further than this and claim to be able to pinpoint an offender's likely home base to within a few streets. In most cases, offenders have been found to live close to the centre of the circle that encompasses all their offences rather than near the edge.

Such knowledge may not necessarily be new to the police. Many officers might claim that it is 'obvious' that an offender is likely to live quite close to their chosen targets. However, techniques such as those advocated by Rossmo and Canter provide for the statistical analysis of data as opposed to relying on hunches or presumptions. The techniques appear to be suited particularly to serial offenders, especially those involved in committing serious sexual assaults. In such cases the police may be at a loss to know where they should start looking for a likely offender. Analysis of the pattern of offences will provide valuable information as to the perpetrator's most probable home base. We should, however, bear in mind one important point. Such predictions rely on the geographical profiler having at their disposal information about each and every offence that forms part of a series. As we noted earlier, it is quite possible that not all victims will have reported their victimisation to the police or that the police will not have recorded the details accurately.

Offender profiling

Offender (or psychological) profiling provides perhaps one of the best examples of the way in which psychology can be applied to police work (Ainsworth, 2001). Unfortunately there are a number of misconceptions as to what offender profiling involves. Some of these misunderstandings stem from fictional portrayals of profilers such as those in the film *The Silence of the Lambs*, and in the British television series *Cracker* in which the main character (Fitz) is invariably shown providing insight into an offender's motives and 'cracking' cases that the police are having difficulty solving. Fitz's methods of working and powers of deduction would, however, alarm most psychologists.

True offender profiling attempts to provide information about an offender's characteristics based upon the careful study of offence characteristics. Within this basic definition, however, there are a number of different approaches. Furthermore, as we will see later, there is disagreement amongst profilers as to the best way to conduct profiling.

We will start our review with an examination of the first developments in the field of profiling that took place in the USA.

The FBI's approach

The earliest systematic approach to profiling was developed by the FBI in the 1970s. Faced with a large number of serial rapes and homicides in the USA, the FBI considered whether it might be possible to glean some information about the sort of person who commits these types of crime and, as a result, the sort of person who should be sought. The FBI believed that the technique might be suited particularly to those crimes in which there was considerable interaction between assailant and victim. The FBI realised that in many crimes it was fairly easy to guess who might be responsible. Most murders, for example, are committed by people who are already known to the victim and in many cases are members of the same family. However, in crimes such as stranger rapes the police may have little idea where they should start looking or, more importantly, of the characteristics that the perpetrator is likely to possess.

The FBI accumulated data on serial offenders from a number of sources. Perhaps most interesting was their decision to carry out in-depth interviews with some 36 convicted serial murderers. The main purpose of these interviews was to identify the major personality dimensions that might be found in this type of offender and to determine how these offenders' personalities differed from those of the normal population. Based on what they had learned, the FBI advocated that investigators should pay close attention to a number of aspects of the crimes under investigation. These included such things as the nature of the attack, the type of victim selected, the crime scene itself, information from the medical examiner's report, and any forensic evidence. The FBI came to realise that whilst the police went to great lengths to obtain physical evidence from the crime scene (e.g. sperm samples or hair) a great deal of other information could be gleaned by a more psychological examination. Such study is generally referred to as crime scene analysis and often forms the basis of any profiling attempt.

Examining these factors allowed FBI profilers to identify the sort of person who was most likely to have committed a certain type of attack. Following their early analysis they were able to suggest a distinction between two types of offenders, i.e. the organised and the disorganised type. As the name implies, organised offenders committed acts that showed clear signs of planning and organisation. For example, their choice of victim would have been pre-planned, they may have brought a weapon with them and would have been careful to avoid leaving any forensic clues. By way of contrast, the disorganised offender would be more likely to select any available target as a victim, use whatever he found at the scene as a weapon, and make little attempt to conceal any forensic evidence.

This distinction was seen to be an important one as it was claimed that the two different types of offender had quite different personalities. Thus if the police were hunting an organised offender they would be looking for one 'type' of person, whereas if they believed that a disorganised offender was involved, their search would lead them in a different direction. In the case of an organised offender, the police would be searching for someone who was quite intelligent, socially skilled, sexually competent, and probably living an apparently respectable life with a partner. By contrast the disorganised offender would be more likely to live alone, to be socially and sexually inept, and to suffer from some quite serious form of mental illness. Such an offender was most likely to commit his offences when in a confused or frightened state.

Use of this typology allowed the police to know what sort of person they should start looking for and, in many cases, to establish whether a series of attacks was likely to be the work of one offender or several. It also allowed predictions to be made regarding if or when the offender was likely to strike again. The linking of similar offences could be important, as it would allow the police to pool any evidence that they did have about individual offences and provide a better picture of the person most likely to be involved.

The FBI's profiling attempts did not stop with the organised/ disorganised typology. Further work allowed them to make other distinctions, e.g. between selfish and pseudo-unselfish rapists (Hazelwood, 1987). Here again the belief was that such distinctions would be of benefit to the police as not only would they allow offences to be linked, but they would also provide insights into the sort of person most likely to be involved. FBI personnel investigated rapes in even more detail and examined the apparent motivation for the assault. This allowed a further classification to be made according to the primary purpose that the rape served for the offender. Thus rapists were further subdivided into separate types, i.e. *power-reassurance*, *power-assertive*, *anger-retaliatory* and *anger-excitement*. Once again the belief was that the different types of rape were likely to be committed by different types of individual and this information would help the police in their search for the perpetrator. If, for example, the police had three possible suspects for a series of rapes, an examination of the nature of the attacks might lead profilers to be able to suggest which of the three was the most likely to have committed the offences.

The FBI is perhaps largely responsible for the development of profiling as we know it today. However, the approach that they took has come in for a great deal of criticism (see for example Rossmo, 1996; Canter and Alison, 1999). Amongst the criticisms is the fact that their system was based on a relatively small sample of US convicted serial killers. Thus it is difficult to say whether their typologies apply to other offenders in other countries. However, most of the criticism has centred on the FBI's reluctance to carry out any kind of systematic evaluation of their work. Despite the fact that the FBI has trained a large number of profilers from different countries, it is all but impossible to establish how valid and reliable their classification systems are. Is it true for example that all organised offenders fit the profile that the FBI have produced? Is it even possible to be certain whether acts committed in a certain way do 'prove' that we are dealing with an organised offender? Critics have even claimed that two different profilers visiting the same crime scene may come up with a different conclusion as regards how the offender should be classified. It also appears to be the case that not all offenders fit neatly into the classification system devised by the FBI. For example, some offenders display behaviours that might fit both sets of criteria and be classified as 'mixed' (Wilson et al, 1997).

One of the most worrying criticisms of the FBI's approach is that a great deal of what is claimed to be 'psychological profiling' has little to do with psychology and is essentially subjective speculation (Canter and Alison, 1999). Certainly reading the memoirs of those who have worked within the FBI's profiling unit (e.g. Douglas and Olshaker, 1995) leaves one wondering whether profiling is an art or a science. Most accounts published to date would lead one to support the former alternative. Critics do not necessarily say that the FBI have got everything wrong; rather they suggest that is all but impossible to either prove or disprove their 'theories'. As has been noted elsewhere:

> Although the FBI's approach to profiling has considerable intuitive appeal it is all but impossible to assess its real value objectively or scientifically.
>
> (Ainsworth, 2001: 113)

Until such time as the FBI lay open their methods and conclusions to scientific scrutiny and peer evaluation, suspicion may remain as to the value of their claims. The FBI's reluctance to open up their work to scientific scrutiny stands in marked contrast to the approach taken by most psychologists. Psychologists typically pride themselves on a strict adherence to scientific principles and objectivity in their research. Following the carrying out of carefully planned and controlled experiments, researchers will open up their work to public scrutiny in order that others can verify or challenge their claims. This is typically done by the publishing of the results of research in academic journals. Such a process allows theories to be challenged, modified, or in some cases rejected. It is the FBI's failure to allow their work to be evaluated in this way that has caused writers such as David Canter to be so critical of the whole approach. We will consider the alternative in the next section.

Investigative psychology and the work of David Canter

In contrast to the FBI, David Canter's starting point is from within the discipline of psychology. Canter brings to profiling a desire for objectivity and the adoption of the scientific method of enquiry. In fact he prefers not to use the term 'profiling' but rather labels his own work *investigative psychology*. Canter's early research was in the area of environmental psychology and a number of concepts and ideas from this field are carried over into his more recent research.

As with any other research psychologist, Canter believes in the generation of hypotheses and the subsequent testing of these hypotheses through experimentation and statistical analysis. Thus, unlike the FBI's approach, Canter does not believe in producing untested notions and presuming them to be valid. As with other fields of scientific enquiry, Canter tries to remove subjectivity from his work and only makes claims once he has demonstrated that his findings have statistical significance. This approach stands in marked contrast to many other examples of 'profiling' in which it is assumed that experience is in itself a guarantee of accuracy.

Canter's early work led him to investigate a number of serious sexual assault cases in the UK (Canter and Heritage, 1990). Through statistical analysis he was able to demonstrate that whilst there were a number of behaviours that were common to most offences, there were others that occurred much less frequently. Canter suggested that a detailed examination of these idiosyncratic behaviours might allow conclusions to be drawn about the perpetrator. Canter believed strongly that the way in which a perpetrator behaves during the commission of any crime will be a reflection of the way in which they behave in everyday life. Thus if a rapist appears to act in a cold and unfeeling manner towards his victim we might expect to find that the rest of his life is characterised by coldness and a lack of intimacy.

Canter believed that as people grow up they learn to interact with the world in certain ways. Each individual may have built up their own behavioural repertoire as a result of these interactions and will have developed certain distinctive behavioural patterns. Ainsworth (2001: 139) has likened this to the default settings in computer programmes in which, unless the computer is told to do something different, it will revert back to its default setting and 'behave' predictably. Canter's research led him to believe that a great deal could be learned by a careful and detailed analysis of the way in which the offender behaved whilst committing the assault. He suggested that attention should be paid in particular to a number of dimensions, i.e. sexuality, violence and aggression, impersonal sexual gratification, interpersonal intimacy, and criminality.

Canter argued that studying these dimensions would allow workers to identify the variations between offenders and, as a result to come closer to identifying the person responsible. However, unlike the FBI, Canter did not believe in trying to place offenders into rigid typologies. Rather his detailed analysis of offence behaviour allowed him to identify which acts were distinctive and which were common. He was also able to identify which acts tended to occur together and which had little relationship with each other. For example, it may be that the use of a weapon and the use of a disguise commonly occur together, whereas the use of a weapon and apologising to the victim do not.

Canter uses a statistical technique that allows the relationship between variables to be examined. This is known as *smallest space analysis* (SSA). Using such a technique allows Canter and other researchers to develop quite sophisticated models of offence behaviour and in particular to identify characteristics that might be peculiar to one offence or one offender. Whilst the police may be used to examining the way in which offenders carry out their crime (i.e. their *modus operandi*) Canter goes beyond this and considers how the way in which the offender carries out his attacks gives us information about the sort of person who was responsible. For example, an offender who blindfolds his victim, wears a disguise, and removes DNA evidence following the attack may be more likely to have a previous criminal history than would a perpetrator who makes no attempt to conceal his identity.

Canter's approach and techniques stand in marked contrast to those of many others involved in profiling (e.g. Britton, 2000). In Canter's work, speculation and presumption are largely rejected in favour of scientific methodology and detailed statistical analysis. While not all have followed Canter's lead, the careful analysis of offence behaviour has led to some useful developments. For example, Kendall *et al* (1999) have suggested that a detailed examination of speech styles of rapists can reveal a great deal about the perpetrator. These researchers suggest that the verbal behaviour exhibited during a rape may be 'typical' of their speech style in everyday life. It has also been found that certain speech styles are associated with variables such as age, employment and the type and number of previous convictions.

We can see from this brief review of the FBI's approach and that of David Canter that there are marked differences between the routes taken by different workers in the field. In some ways the difference may be a reflection of a more general difference in the approach of law enforcement personnel and psychologists. Whilst those working within law enforcement may gather information and reproduce their ideas with little attention to notions of reliability and validity, the approach of the trained psychologist will be somewhat different. However, the approach of psychologists may be more likely to allow us to identify which profiling techniques might be the most useful and, most importantly, why. Currently the world of profiling is a divided one in which advocates of different approaches pour scorn upon the approaches of others. At the heart of the debate is the question of whether profiling should be seen as an art or a science. If profiling is to become an accepted 'science' it will be necessary for those working in the field to use an approach that mirrors those used in the natural and the social sciences. If this is done it is perhaps more likely that the true value and potential of profiling for police work will be realised.

Summary

We have seen in this chapter that the police can learn a great deal by the careful analysis of crime occurrences and crime patterns. Systematic analysis allows us to identify hot-spots of crime and, in some cases to identify the reasons why such hot-spots occur. We have also seen that psychology can add to the police's understanding in a number of ways. One of the best examples of this is the study of repeat victimisation. Understanding how common repeat victimisation is and the reasons for its occurrence allows the police to better target their resources and to identify future victims of crime.

We have also seen in this chapter that profiling may have something to offer the police, in particular by focusing on the actions of offenders when committing their crimes. Although there are strong differences of opinion as to how profiling should be conducted, some of the techniques already in use do offer interesting insights into offenders' behaviour. In cases where the police have little idea where they should start looking for an offender, profiling can be a valuable tool. However, profiling represents just one small part of the role that psychologists might play in the investigation of serious crime (Jackson *et al*, 1997). There remains some misunderstanding as to what profiling is and what it can achieve. Psychologists will need to address these misconceptions if they are to challenge some of the misgivings held by many police officers.

Psychologists and profilers should also be aware of the potential misuses of profiling. It should be remembered that profiling can at best identify some of the characteristics that an offender is likely to possess. It cannot state whether one particular person did or did not commit the crime under investigation. This is an important point. Most profilers would recoil in horror if the police were to arrest a particular individual simply because he matched the profile that had been provided to them. Most courts do not currently accept 'expert' evidence from profilers (Gudjonsson and Haward, 1998: 173) and it may be some time until profiling has reached the stage where this situation will be reversed.

Further reading

Ainsworth, P. B. (2001) *Offender Profiling and Crime Analysis.* Cullompton: Willan Publishing.

Canter, D. and Alison, L. (1999) *Profiling in Policy and Practice.* Aldershot: Ashgate.

Jackson, J. L. and Bekerian, D. A. (eds.) (1997) *Offender Profiling: Theory, Research and Practice.* Chichester: Wiley.

Chapter 10

Hostage taking and negotiation

One area in which psychology appears already to have proved useful to policing is in the field of hostage taking and subsequent negotiation. These types of incidents are thankfully rare; however, when they do occur they can pose very real problems for both the police and the hostages. As we saw in Chapter 1, psychology has much to offer in understanding communication, and cases involving hostage negotiation allow special communication skills to be developed and employed. Although we will be talking mainly of situations in which hostages are being held, many of the principles underlying negotiation will apply in cases known as 'barricades' in which an individual is barricaded away and is threatening to harm him/herself. In what follows we will examine some of the ways in which psychology may be of help in dealing with this difficult area.

Types of hostage situations

There are a number of reasons why hostages might be taken. The main types of incidents that are likely to be encountered are:

1. Crimes that have 'gone wrong' in that criminals have been unable to escape and have ended up taking hostages.

2. Incidents whereby a hostage is taken and a ransom demanded, the primary motive being financial gain.

3. Incidents in which hostages are taken for mainly political purposes and in order to achieve some political end.

4. Domestic incidents in which one member of the family holds others hostage and threatens to harm others and perhaps him/herself.

5. Incidents in which individuals with a mental disorder take hostage people who they believe may be trying to harm them or against whom they have some kind of grudge.

6. Prison riots in which hostages are taken and demands made.

Although this probably represents the major types of incident, the categories are not mutually exclusive and may overlap. Nevertheless it is important to understand that there are a number of different types of hostage situations, each of which may have its own characteristics and dangers. The 'rules' by which each person in the hostage drama plays will differ significantly from one type of incident to another. Tactics that are useful in one type of incident may be less successful in another. Nevertheless as we will see in this chapter, there are a number of useful strategies and techniques that can be employed across different types of hostage situation.

Responding to hostage situations

Hostage negotiation is a specialised skill that is best carried out by those who have received adequate training and have built up experience in dealing with this type of incident. Nevertheless the reality is that the first on the scene of such an incident may well be a uniformed patrol officer with little if any experience of dealing with situations of this kind. The first officer on the scene can have an impact on the course of the situation and it is important that this officer does as little as possible to make the situation worse. Obvious examples would be further enraging an already distraught hostage-taker, or putting the person in a position whereby killing the hostages and perhaps him/herself seems like the best option. Noesner and Nolan (1992) have offered some advice as to how those first on the scene might best act. Much of this advice is concerned with ensuring the safety of the officer and those held, although other suggestions emphasise the need for the officer to do as little as possible in order not to inflame a delicate situation.

While police officers may be used to 'wading in' and dealing with incidents themselves, in this type of situation this course of action will rarely be appropriate. Indeed developments in the field of negotiation stem largely from an acknowledgement in the 1970s that there were alternative ways of dealing with such incidents, which did not involve the use of (often deadly) force. In one case in 1971 the FBI's decision to storm a plane resulted in the death of two hostages and a hijacker. The intervention was followed by litigation in which it was claimed that the decision by the incident commander to use force was inappropriate (see Downs v U.S., 1975; Higginbotham, 1994). The new approach that was developed as an alternative to the use of force still stressed containment and an assessment of threat, but also emphasised how time and negotiation could be used effectively (McMains and Mullins, 1996).

Techniques used by negotiators

One of the things that negotiators will try to do is to present a model of calm behaviour to the hostage-taker. In doing so it is hoped that the hostage-taker will emulate this form of communication and a much better dialogue ensue. The first officer on the scene would do well to remember this and should avoid raising the temperature any further by shouting or behaving aggressively. The gathering of as much accurate information as possible about the incident, the hostage-taker and the hostages will be the most useful contribution that the first responder can make.

The Los Angeles Police Department have some of the best-developed and most experienced hostage negotiation teams. Their mantra is 'Talk to me'. This sounds like such a simple notion yet it underpins a great deal of what the teams try to do. Thus one of the first objectives will be to establish communication with the hostage-taker and listen to what they have to say. There will be ample time later to use negotiation skills in which the person might be persuaded to do certain things, but for now the most important thing is simply to listen to what the person has to say. It is important from the outset that the negotiator tries to establish good communication and a rapport with the hostage-taker by, for example, using first names. Hatcher et al (1998: 455) suggest that the basis of the approach used in this type of incident can be described thus:

> Emotionality is driving the situation and the emotion-based solution that the hostage-taker or barricaded suspect chooses to resolve his/her problem can be shifted or modified given the right verbal and/or tactical strategy.

Although we will refer throughout this chapter to 'the negotiator' it should be noted that there will in fact be a number of people who make up the negotiating team. Typically there will be the primary negotiator, who establishes communication with the hostage-taker, but there will also be a secondary negotiator or 'coach' who can advise the primary negotiator or offer suggestions as to how to conduct the sessions. The reasoning here is that the primary negotiator may find it difficult to both talk to the hostage-taker and plan a strategy. By dividing up the tasks, the primary negotiator can concentrate on rapport building while someone else can stand back and monitor what is happening and suggest things that might be tried next. There will also be a scribe or journalist on the team who will monitor and record everything that is being said. The team will also often include a psychologist or mental health professional, especially in cases where the hostage-taker appears to be suffering from a mental disorder.

The role of the psychologist

McMains (1988) identified three roles that a psychologist can take in hostage negotiations, i.e. professional, consultant and participant observer. In the last of these the psychologist will tend to act as part of the team and offer advice or make observations via the secondary negotiator. In this scenario the psychologist may be able to identify and assess the various needs of the hostage-taker and offer advice on appropriate ways to build rapport. Those who believe that the psychologist's role in all this is a glamorous one may wish to heed the comments of Super (1999: 415) who suggests that:

> Psychologists may serve negotiators in any way that may be of assistance to them: from providing coffee and getting a coat, to scripting different approaches the negotiator may use.

Borum (1988) suggests that, whilst psychologists can provide useful advice to the team in terms of the negotiation, they may not be as effective as well-trained and experienced law enforcement personnel in conducting the negotiation itself. This particular research concentrated on scenarios involving mentally disturbed hostage-takers and it is unclear whether the same may hold true with other types of negotiations. Hatcher et al (1998) suggest that there are a number of different roles that psychologists can play, i.e.:

- Consultant/adviser
- Integrated team member

- Primary negotiator
- Primary controller.

There are both advantages and disadvantages to the different uses of psychologists in each of these roles. However, Hatcher *et al* make the point that police officers will not necessarily welcome psychologists with open arms. These writers suggest that psychologists may have to wait to be invited to join the negotiation team and that such an invitation will depend upon mutual acceptance, professional credibility and an ability to function in the field. Police officers often maintain a high level of cynicism about the contribution that 'outsiders' can make and, as a result, a psychologist who claims to be an expert will need to prove him/herself before being accepted and gaining respect from police officers. As Hatcher *et al* (1998: 462) note:

> The psychologist's credibility most often depends on the ability to provide critical, rather than just interesting, information.

Nevertheless, psychologists have been responsible for developing and evaluating many of the strategies currently employed in hostage situations (Butler *et al*, 1993). Psychologists may also have a contribution to make by helping the police to identify the sort of person who would make a good negotiator. For example, Getty and Elam (1988) used psychometric tests to identify those who would make successful negotiators. They found that successful negotiators had good verbal skills, a positive self-image, good reasoning ability and a high sensitivity to others. It also seems an obvious point that those who do not generally cope well with stressful situations are unlikely to perform well as negotiators.

The negotiating team and their responsibilities

Because the negotiator and coach will tend to be wrapped up in the negotiation itself, it is important that there is another person who can monitor progress and provide an objective view of the state of the situation. Thus a decision regarding if and when an attempt will be made to rescue the hostages will not be taken by the negotiators themselves. One reason why this might be important is that, in establishing good communication with the hostage-taker, the negotiator will build up a relationship with the person to a point where an objective assessment of what should be done becomes more difficult. It is often said that when one is embroiled in a tense situation it is difficult to step back and see the bigger picture. During the negotiations, the negotiator may start to empathise with the hostage-taker and not want to see them harmed even though they pose a real threat to others. Although the emphasis will be on negotiation and a peaceful resolution of the incident, there will need to be a back-up team of police officers who can make a rescue attempt at short notice, should this prove necessary.

The negotiator will encourage the hostage-taker to reveal why they have done what they have done, what it is that is distressing them at this point in time, and how they came to be in the position in which they now find themselves. Although the emphasis is on listening to the hostage-taker, the negotiator would use what are referred to as *active listening skills*. In doing this the negotiator lets the hostage-taker know that they are hearing what is being said, but also that they understand and are interested in what the person has to say. Active listening skills would include repeating what the person has said in order that the person knows that they have been both heard and understood. The negotiator will try to reinforce the hostage-taker each time they speak so that they are more likely to carry on speaking. They can also encourage more talking by asking open-ended questions (that require a lengthy response) rather than closed questions that can be answered with a simple yes or no. Asking the person to talk about how they are feeling will tend to produce a fuller response than simply asking, 'Are you scared?'

The primary goal at this stage is the development of a personal relationship between negotiator and hostage-taker. Although 'the negotiator' will in reality be a team of people, it is considered important that only one person communicates with the hostage-taker directly. If members of the team need to communicate with the negotiator, they will do so by writing notes rather than speaking in order that the hostage-taker will continue to presume that there is a simple one-to-one conversation taking place. Steps will also be taken to ensure that there are no distractions (e.g. from police radios or telephones) so that once again the hostage-taker will come to believe that a genuine one-to-one communication is taking place.

Establishing good communication with the hostage-taker means that the person's exact needs and demands can be established. In some cases the hostage-taker will be very clear and specific about what they want, but in others the person may be confused and imprecise. It is, however, important that the negotiator has a clear idea of what it is that the person hopes to get out of the situation. A hostage situation can be characterised as one in which the hostage-taker is trying to gain something. The taking of hostages gives the hostage-taker power and can thus be a reinforcer in itself. For someone who normally feels powerless and has little influence in the world, taking hostages can bring immediate rewards in terms of the person suddenly receiving a great deal of attention.

In some of the examples listed above it will be clear that the hostage-taker wants something that they do not currently have and that the negotiator has it within their power to secure this for the hostage-taker. Thus the foiled bank robbers who find themselves trapped in the bank with a number of employee-hostages may demand a helicopter in order to make good their escape. However, in many other cases the 'needs' of the hostage-taker will be much less specific. In some situations, simply knowing that the world is now aware of their grievance will be sufficient to make the hostage-taker feel that they have achieved something by their actions. Nevertheless the negotiator will need to persuade the hostage-taker that continuing to talk will lead to further 'achievements'.

Negotiators will try to employ a number of techniques that are related to the 'active listening' strategy introduced above. For example, they may use emotional labelling in which they say to the person 'you sound very angry right now' and encourage the person to talk about this. Encouraging the person to talk can, over the course of time, wear them down, although in this case getting them to talk about their feelings serves another purpose. Allowing the person to talk about what they are feeling inserts another step between thinking about the issues and acting upon them. Once a person has told another why they are angry and has had their grievances listened to, a more normal and rational conversation becomes more likely. Although many hostage-takers will be in an angry and agitated state they may also be experiencing a great deal of anxiety about their situation and how it can be resolved. If the negotiator is able to lower the person's anxiety levels, it will prove easier to have a rational conversation and to reason with the individual. The core purpose of this stage of the negotiation is to delay or ideally to prevent the hostage-taker from acting impulsively. In doing so it becomes less likely that the hostage-taker will act violently or aggressively.

Time is on the side of the negotiators and one of the most important qualities that they will need is patience. As noted earlier, playing the waiting game may not come naturally to many police officers. They will be used to responding to calls as quickly as possible and to taking swift action on arrival at an incident. These tendencies must, however, be reined in and the waiting game be allowed to play itself out. There is obviously great variation in the length of time that different types of hostage situations take to resolve. However, the average time taken to end these types of incidents is between six and eight hours. Of course some incidents can go on for several days, and can test the patience of the most patient of negotiators. It does, however, appear that if an incident lasts for more than five or six days, little is likely to be achieved by negotiation beyond that point. By this stage, all parties will tend to have reached entrenched positions and are unlikely to shift their stance no matter how long the incident continues.

It may be inappropriate to challenge the hostage-taker at an early stage with regard to some of their beliefs. In cases involving mentally disturbed individuals what may well be a delusion (e.g. about others persecuting the person) will appear very real to the individual concerned. Rapport is unlikely if the negotiator immediately challenges the hostage-taker over what may be their core beliefs. Dealing with people who have a serious mental disorder presents its own challenges and in such cases the advice of a psychiatrist or clinical psychologist is essential.

Part of the reason why it is important to monitor the course of the negotiation is to check whether things are progressing in a positive or a negative direction. Although the aim of the hostage negotiator is to bring the incident to a peaceful resolution, there will be times when this is simply not possible. Constant monitoring allows a decision to be made as to when negotiation must stop and action be taken. If, for example, the hostage-taker threatens to kill one hostage at a set time and shows no sign of changing this intention an operational decision will need to be made. Negotiators must be conscious of any 'time imperatives' that the hostage-taker is working around and try to have these changed. Similarly if the situation appears to be moving closer to what is referred to as a 'violent action imperative' (where the hostage-taker feels compelled to act) a quick decision will need to be taken.

Problem solving and defusion of the situation

Once things have calmed down a little the negotiator will try to move on to the problem-solving phase of negotiations. In some cases the negotiator may suggest certain courses of action to the hostage-taker but he/she may also ask the hostage-taker for suggestions as to what might be done next. In some cases the hostage-taker may be more likely to do certain things if they believe that it was their own idea. However, in other situations (e.g. where the person is so distressed that they cannot think rationally) it will be up to the negotiator to suggest a course of action. If the negotiator has been successful in establishing a good rapport, then the hostage-taker is much more likely to accede to the negotiator's wishes.

The negotiator and the rest of the team may well have a plan that they can work to in order to achieve their eventual objective. They do, however, need to have a good understanding of the dynamics of the situation and the way in which a successful resolution is likely to be achieved. They may, for example, decide which areas they want the hostage-taker to talk about and which they do not want to discuss. They should have thought ahead to how they will respond to requests that the hostage-taker is likely to make. If, for example, the hostage-taker asks that a relative be brought to the scene, the negotiator will need to have an answer ready. In some cases, allowing the hostage-taker to speak to a relative may be helpful, but in most cases it will not. One problem with doing this is that the negotiator loses some control over the situation if they allow the hostage-taker to speak directly to another person. Having worked hard on developing a good relationship and in achieving some degree of control, the negotiator would need to think carefully before allowing a third person to be introduced into the interaction. If the negotiator does agree to this, it is advisable that the relative be advised as to what should or should not be said.

In the scenario described above we are starting to look at demands and concessions. As noted at the start of the chapter, hostage-takers do what they do for a reason and may have a firm idea of what they hope to achieve. Whilst perhaps stalling on the demands that the hostage-taker is making, the negotiator may offer smaller concessions in order to gain the trust of the hostage-taker. This can be important for a number of reasons. Firstly a negotiator who is perceived to be unhelpful and unwilling to do anything for the hostage-taker is not really 'negotiating' at all. However, if the perception is of a negotiator who may be willing to allow small requests, then a better relationship is more likely. In many cases it will be inappropriate to rule out any requests outright, but the negotiator will need to find a way of avoiding a direct response to some demands. This can be achieved by, for example, the negotiator saying that he/she will need to discuss the request with a senior officer or to consult with other authorities.

The second reason why allowing some concessions can be important is that the negotiator can use this as a form of bargaining tool. The negotiator may, for example, agree to a request for food to be delivered but only in return for some concession on the part of the hostage-taker. Thus one hostage may be released in exchange for the provision of food and drinks. We must bear in mind a point made earlier in respect of power and control. Although the hostage-taker is in a position of power in the sense that he/she has control over the fate of the hostages, the negotiator also has some degree of power and control over other things that the hostage-taker may want. The provision of food and drink is one obvious example, but there may be other things (e.g. the restoration of electrical power to a building) which might be used as bargaining chips.

The foot-in-the-door and other techniques

Persuading the hostage-taker to do even one small thing is an important first step. There is a fairly well established principle in social psychology, which is concerned with the so-called 'foot-in-the-door' technique (Freedman and Fraser, 1966). This refers to the fact that if you wish someone to do you a large favour, you would be well advised to start by asking them a very small favour. Salespeople often employ this technique. Thus the door-to-door salesman does not open with a request that you buy £20,000 worth of double-glazing from his company. Far more likely will be a simple request for you to answer one or two innocent sounding questions. The skilled sales person will then gradually increase the demands that are made on you until the eventual 'signing on the dotted line'. The demands should be in such small increments that each new request is not perceived to be a large step up from the previous one. The bottom line in all this is that if someone does agree to a small request they are significantly more likely to agree to other larger requests. Having done one small favour, there is some pressure on the individual to do further 'favours'. In effect it provides justification in advance for agreeing to the larger request. As Aronson (1999: 197) notes:

> Escalation is self-perpetuating. Once a small commitment is made it sets the stage for ever-increasing commitments.

One reason why the foot-in-the-door technique works is that people generally like their behaviours to be consistent. Thus agreeing to do something for someone else is likely to be followed by agreement to do something additional if the same person makes a similar request in future. There is also an element of self-justification here. For example, if you find yourself giving a sum of money to a charity you may justify your actions by saying that it is a worthwhile cause or that the person who made the request for a donation seemed like a 'very nice' person and you felt good about helping them. However, you may also justify your actions by saying that you gave to the charity because you are a generous sort of a person who believes that it is right to help others less fortunate than yourself. If this is how you explain your actions it does of course mean that future requests, even if they are made by a different charity, will be more likely to be agreed to. It is for this reason that some charities are eager to obtain lists of people who have already made donations to other charities.

Returning to our discussion of hostage situations, the negotiator can use the fact that the hostage-taker has agreed to a small request in future discussions. The negotiator may suggest to the hostage-taker that they are actually quite a compassionate person in that they did agree to let one terrified hostage go. The negotiator may play on the fact that, in order to maintain behavioural consistency, the hostage-taker should consider letting others go. If it is handled correctly, the ultimate act of surrender may be perceived as just one additional small step along a continuum of conformity. However, in order to achieve this, the negotiator will need to have convinced the hostage-taker that by surrendering they will not lose face completely, and may still maintain some dignity. As things start to move in a hostage negotiation, the hostage-taker's demands may become less and less important to them. In this case, the ending of the incident without being harmed by the police will then take on much greater significance.

Although the foot-in-the-door technique appears to be well established, an alternative is the so-called 'door in the face' method (Cialdini *et al*, 1975). According to this viewpoint, if you wish someone to do a small favour for you it may be worthwhile asking for an extremely large and unreasonable favour first. Although you can be almost certain that this large request will be refused, if it is followed immediately by a much smaller request, the latter may be agreed to as it is so trivial compared with the initial outlandish request. Thus if you want a friend to lend you £5 you may start by asking them if they can lend you £1000. If the refusal is followed immediately by a request for £5 it may well be forthcoming. One may again relate this to the hostage situation. If the hostage-taker laughs at the suggestion that they should release all of the large number of hostages being held, they may see a request to release just one person as almost trivial by comparison.

Does negotiation work?

The sorts of tactics described in this chapter appear to have a high success rate. In their recent review, Hatcher *et al* (1998: 456) state that almost 75%

of these events are resolved through negotiated surrender, and fewer than 10% result in loss of life of the perpetrator through lethal force or suicide. Furthermore in another study it was found that only 3% of hostage incidents resulted in the killing of a hostage by the hostage-taker (Butler *et al*, 1993). The problem with such figures is that it is all but impossible to establish whether the successful resolution of the incident can be attributed entirely to the tactics and skills of the negotiation team. For example, it is possible that some proportion of hostage-takers would surrender anyway, irrespective of what was done or said by negotiators. Skilled negotiation involves the use of a large number of tactics, many of which are based on established psychological principles. Each of these techniques may well contribute something to the eventual outcome of the incident, but it would be all but impossible to demonstrate which particular technique was the most influential in a successful outcome.

As you will have seen throughout this book, psychologists often test their hypotheses by conducting carefully controlled experiments in the laboratory. The advantage of this approach is that it allows the researcher to control any extraneous factors and to investigate each variable systematically. Thus in the case of hostage situations a researcher might investigate separately a range of techniques used routinely in negotiations in order to establish which was successful and why. Of course in the real-life world of hostage negotiations, such 'luxuries' are not possible. Hostage negotiation skills have been built up over many years, partly as a result of trial and error. Many of the techniques employed do, however, have their origins in carefully controlled psychological research.

A systematic evaluation of each component of the strategy used in the field would provide further information that could be invaluable to future negotiations. Knowing that something works is obviously important but equally it would be helpful to know *why* it worked and whether any refinements or improvements are possible. It is routine to hold debriefing sessions after each incident and to review the success (or failure) of the operation. However, a more systematic evaluation of the proceedings might allow us to make more confident statements as to the relative utility of different components. In the USA, the FBI have compiled a database of information gleaned from hostage negotiations and it remains to be seen whether this proves useful in refining and improving negotiation techniques.

Hatcher *et al* (1998: 469) suggest that, although hostage negotiation is a specialised skill, those psychologists with an academic and research background could make a valuable contribution to hostage negotiations by:

- Establishing relationships with hostage negotiation teams so that a programme of evaluative research can be carried out.

- Examining the skills and cognitive decision making strategies of successful negotiators and teams.

- Determining the relative contribution of screening and training in the development of successful negotiators.

- Assessing the decision-making processes of the hostage-taker and its relationship to his/her previous life experiences.

- Understanding in more detail the behaviour of hostages (especially where more than one hostage is taken).

Stress and danger in hostage negotiations

We should bear in mind that hostage situations are, by their very nature, tense and dangerous events and all those involved are at risk. Although a negotiation team deserves praise for a successful outcome, the rescued hostages may carry the mental scars of their ordeal for many years. In one study (Vila *et al*, 1999) it was found that many children who had been held hostage in their school were still affected by their ordeal up to 18 months later. In this case, early intervention and careful monitoring were not sufficient to stave off symptoms of post-traumatic stress disorder in many children (see Chapter 8).

We should also bear in mind that negotiators may themselves be traumatised by their experiences. Although some hostage situations will result in harm to hostages and hostage-taker irrespective of what techniques are used, negotiators may feel themselves to be personally responsible for a bad outcome. They may even blame themselves for the death of a hostage despite being reassured that they had done everything that they could. For this reason, careful debriefing and the offer of counselling should be made available to negotiators. If negotiations have been protracted, the negotiator will have built up quite a close relationship with the hostage-taker and, in some cases, with the hostages themselves. As with the break-up of any relationship, adjustment may prove difficult in the short term. If, as in some cases, a negotiator holds him/herself personally responsible, coming to terms with the outcome may prove difficult.

The Stockholm syndrome

One curious finding to emerge from the analysis of hostage situations is that on some occasions the hostages appear to form quite a close attachment to their captors. 'Common sense' might lead us to predict that, once released safely, the hostages would feel a great deal of anger and contempt for their captors. However, in some cases the opposite appears to occur. The title of this syndrome derives from a bank robbery that took place in Stockholm, Sweden (Strentz, 1979). In this case, the robbery went wrong and the robbers took hostages and held them captive in the bank for several days. The situation was eventually resolved peacefully and the robbers arrested. However, when the hostages were questioned about their ordeal, many praised their captors and were concerned that they should not be harmed. Some were even reluctant to testify against their captors when they appeared in court.

At first glance this is a somewhat puzzling phenomenon although Strentz's analysis sheds some light on the reasons for its occurrence. Strentz found that there was a relationship between the length of time that the hostage situation lasted and the likelihood of the development of the Stockholm syndrome. Other important variables appeared to be whether there was positive contact between captor and hostage, and the level of social interaction that took place between these two parties.

From a psychological viewpoint, the reasons for the development of the syndrome are perhaps quite easily understood. Although captor and hostage play very different roles in the scenario, over time, they may begin to share a common fear, i.e. that they will both be harmed or killed. Research carried out on those who survive disasters shows that they often form close bonds with one another following the incident. Facing death together appears to be a powerful catalyst for the development of a close relationship. Providing that the hostage incident ends peacefully, each party may be glad to have survived the ordeal and develop a mutual respect for their co-survivor.

Over time, the scenario becomes less one of hostage/captor but one of a cohesive group of people who need to get themselves out of a tense and difficult situation. In a way, the hostage-taker and the hostages come to form one 'group', whereas all those on the outside comprise a separate 'group' (see Chapter 2). A relationship will have been built up between captor and hostage and the relationship between the two will have changed. For example, over time, the hostage may come to be seen by their captor not just as 'a hostage', but rather as a real person with a name, and perhaps a family. Part of the role of the negotiator will be to try to change the way in which the hostage-taker perceives the hostages, the belief being

163

that this will affect the likelihood of them being harmed. Over time, the hostages themselves may come to see the hostage-taker not as someone who is probably going to kill them, but rather as someone who held their life in their hands, but chose not to end it. In such a case, relief and gratitude may add to the positive feelings directed towards the captor.

The Stockholm syndrome remains an unexpected outcome of some negotiations although its appearance is by no means certain. In a number of cases, hostages feel nothing but hatred for their captors and in some incidents will harm or even kill their captors if given the chance. Nevertheless, what we have learned about the syndrome allows us to predict those situations in which it is likely to occur. In a recent analysis of skyjacking (Slatkin, 1998) it was found that there was a relationship between the development of the syndrome and the variables of time and social interaction. However, in this study, no relationship was found between development of the syndrome and the variable of positive contact between captor and captives (i.e. absence of abuse).

It is important that we understand the dynamics behind the Stockholm syndrome and the variables that are associated with its occurrence. When planning how to end a hostage situation, rescuers cannot assume that the hostages will want to get as far away from their captors as they can as soon as possible. It may be that hostages who show signs of the Stockholm syndrome will emerge alongside their captors, partly to ensure that they are not harmed by the police. In terms of the hostages, they may realise that they could easily have been killed by their captors but were spared. The fact that the hostage-takers chose not to harm the hostages may make it more likely that they will feel gratitude towards their captors and, as a result, not wish to see them harmed. Even after the rescue and the capture of the perpetrator, hostages and hostage-takers may stay in contact by corresponding while the hostage-taker is in prison.

Summary

In this chapter we have seen that the discipline of psychology has a great deal to offer those involved in the delicate art of hostage negotiation. Some of the more successful strategies used in such negotiations are devised from the results of psychological studies that have, in some cases, been carried out in a different context. However, we have noted that law enforcement personnel may not welcome psychologists into their ranks unconditionally. In order to gain acceptance and respect, psychologists need to demonstrate their utility in the field.

As an alternative to the use of force, negotiation is surely an avenue worth exploring. With increasing knowledge and experience of hostage situations, it is now possible to offer guidance on the sorts of techniques that are likely to be successful. Psychology can offer valuable insights into the way in which *all* those involved in this type of situation might behave. For example, Wilson and Smith (2000) suggest that a careful analysis of the rules and roles in terrorist hostage-taking incidents can provide a great deal of useful information. Some of the more unusual characteristics of hostage-taking scenarios (e.g. the Stockholm syndrome) can also be explained by reference to psychological principles. Bearing this in mind it seems likely that psychology's contribution to this burgeoning field will continue to grow.

Further reading

Blau, T. H. (1994) *Psychological Services for Law Enforcement*. New York: Wiley.

Hatcher, C., Mohandie, K., Turner, J. and Gelles, M. G. (1998) The role of the psychologist in crisis/hostage negotiations. *Behavioral Sciences and the Law*, 16, 455-472.

Wilson, M. and Smith, A. (2000) Rules and roles in terrorist hostage taking. In. D. Canter, and L. Alison (eds.) *The Social Psychology of Crime: Groups, Teams and Networks*. Aldershot: Ashgate.

Conclusion

In this volume we have looked at a number of ways in which psychology might be applied profitably to policing. It has been stressed that there are a multitude of areas in which the results of psychological research have relevance for police officers. In recent years there has been a real growth in what has come to be known as 'police psychology'. This has covered well-established areas such as selection and stress, and relatively new areas such as negotiation and hostage taking (Kurke and Scrivner, 1995; Blau, 1994). Whilst development of these fields is important there are perhaps many other areas in which psychology can be of considerable benefit.

It has been argued that as a great deal of policing involves human interaction, psychology is highly relevant to many of the day-to-day situations that police officers face. However, where psychology has been brought into police work it has generally not been at this 'grass roots' level. For example, while there have been some attempts to introduce an understanding of good interaction skills, these have not been seen as particularly important to most trainers. Writing one of the first books on psychology and policing (Ainsworth and Pease, 1987) it was argued that psychology had a great deal to offer police officers and a view was expressed that in the following years psychology would play a much greater role in the training of officers. Some 15 years later, there have not been the advances that were hoped for at that time.

While it is true that there are many more police psychologists employed today, the roles that they are filling tend to be somewhat restricted. Many psychologists who come to the work have a background in mental health or in organisational psychology. As a result, a great deal of police psychologists' time is taken up with selection and recruitment issues and with stress counselling. There are, however, a number of other areas where psychology is increasingly useful (e.g. hostage negotiations) and police forces are now more welcoming of inputs in these areas.

In other areas (e.g. psychological profiling) the police have been keen to use any ideas that might be useful, although there has often been disappointment at the results (Ainsworth, 2001). Partly as a result of this, the negative view of psychologists held by many police officers has persisted. There have, however, been some notable successes in the application of psychological work to policing. As we saw in Chapter 9, Ken Pease's pioneering work on repeat victimisation has allowed the police to target their resources better and to make some predictions about where and when crime will occur in the future.

Psychological applications to police work have generally taken two forms. Apart from those psychologists who are working within police organisations, there are many more who are carrying out research that is highly relevant to policing. For example, in Chapters 5 and 6 we saw how an understanding of the processes of perception and memory can help to explain why witnesses (including police officers) can make mistakes. However, psychologists have also developed methods and techniques that might make it less likely that errors will be made by eyewitnesses. The work of Beth Loftus in particular has pointed to the importance of question wording and the need to avoid introducing misleading information.

The cognitive interview technique has also been highly successful in eliciting more information from witnesses than the traditional form of police interviewing. However, as we saw in Chapter 6, the introduction of methods such as investigative interviewing have not always produced the sea change in practice that had been anticipated. As Clarke and Milne (2001) acknowledge, there are a number of hurdles that need to be negotiated before any change will be endorsed and accepted by the rank and file members of the organisation. Nevertheless, recommendations such as those made by Wells *et al* (1998) suggest that improvements can be made in the way in which identification parades and photo-spreads are conducted.

We saw in Chapter 7 that there may be problems associated with the interviewing of suspects. It was argued that police officers' beliefs about suspects might mean that they are unable to assess objectively what takes place in the interview room. Research suggests that some of the techniques employed in interviews may persuade the innocent (especially vulnerable individuals) to confess falsely.

In Chapter 7 we also saw that police officers' beliefs in their ability to detect deception may be ill founded. It appears that, like most members of the public, police officers often rely on inappropriate cues when assessing whether or nor people are lying. Perhaps of most interest to the present discussion is the research by Vrij (2001) that showed that even if a psychologist tries to help police officers to improve their lie detection skills, many reject the advice and fall back on their own (often incorrect) stereotypes. This suggests that psychologists still have some way to go before the value of what they have to offer is recognised!

There are many issues that concern the modern police service. Not least of these are questions of prejudice and discrimination by police officers. Twenty years ago, there were serious riots in parts of the UK and Lord Scarman wrote an influential report that identified prejudice by police officers as one contributory factor. Following the publication of the report, most police forces vowed to change their practices and to root out prejudice from within their ranks. Twenty years later we have seen a number of senior British police officers admitting that there is institutional racism within their organisations. Surely a starting point to any change in attitude and behaviour by police officers is an under-standing of the psychological processes that can lead to prejudice and discrimination. These have been spelled out in Chapter 2.

There are many other important issues that confront society and policing today, one obvious example being the level of aggression and violence. Many police officers will have their own views as to why people behave violently though such viewpoints may not take into account the complexity that can surround this type of behaviour. It was argued in Chapter 4 that a thorough understanding of the psychological factors that can lead to aggressive behaviour is an important first step in trying to reduce these forms of behaviour. We also saw that it may be possible to reduce the level of violence and aggression shown by police officers themselves, providing we understand the reasons for its occurrence.

Nevertheless, it would appear that the potential of psychology has not been fully recognised by many within the police service, despite the efforts of those who are convinced of its value. There are a number of reasons for this, many of which have been explored in this volume. It would be unfair to place the 'blame' for the current state of affairs entirely at the feet of police organisations. Psychologists have not always gone out of their way to understand the needs of law enforcement agencies nor have they found the time needed to convince the sceptical of the value of their 'product'. White and Honig (1995: 259) suggest that 'It is unlikely that the field of law enforcement will ever fully embrace the field of psychology'. Such a view does not, however, mean that psychologists could not do more to win over the doubters.

Martin Reisser was one of the pioneers of police psychology working with the LAPD in California for many years. Reflecting on his years of experience he says:

> Managers who recognize the pragmatic value of psychological insights in the welter of police-related contexts have come to view the police psychologist as a valued partner with the special expertise essential to cost-effective planning and decision making. Both professions, police and psychology, have learned much from each other in their collaborative interaction.
>
> (Reisser, 1995: xiii)

It is to be hoped that those police officers who have read this book may be a little more convinced of the value of psychology within the police setting. It is also hoped that any psychologists who read this volume will feel that policing is one arena in which their contribution can be of value. Law enforcement is an important issue for all societies and any knowledge that might contribute to a more efficient and effective police service is surely to be welcomed.

References

Addison, K. S. (2000) *A Comparison of the Performance of Graduate and Non-Graduate Recruit Police Officers During Their Stage 2 Training at a Police Training Centre.* Unpublished M. A. thesis, University of Manchester.

Ainsworth, P. B. (2001) *Offender Profiling and Crime Analysis.* Cullompton: Willan.

Ainsworth, P. B. (2000) *Psychology and Crime: Myths and Reality.* Harlow: Longman.

Ainsworth, P. B. (1998a) *Psychology, Law and Eyewitness Testimony.* Chichester: Wiley.

Ainsworth, P. B. (1998b) Police folklore and attributions of guilt: Can psychology challenge long held assumptions? In J. Baros, I. Munnich and M. Szegedi (eds.) *Psychology and Criminal Justice: International Review of Theory and Research.* Berlin: Walter de Guyter.

Ainsworth, P. B. (1996) Psychological testing and police recruit selection: Difficulties and dilemmas. In G. Davies, S. Lloyd-Bostock, M. McMurran and C. Wilson (eds.) *Psychology, Law and Criminal Justice: International Developments in Research and Practice.* Berlin: Walter de Gruyter.

Ainsworth, P. B. (1995) *Psychology and Policing in a Changing World.* Chichester: Wiley.

Ainsworth, P. B. and King, E. (1988) Witnesses' perceptions of identification parades. In M. M. Gruneberg, P. E. Morris and R. N. Sykes (eds.) *Practical Aspects of Memory: Current Research and Issues, Vol. 1.* Chichester: Wiley.

Ainsworth, P. B. and May, G. (1996) Obtaining information from traumatised witnesses through the CIT. Paper presented to the *Trauma and Memory Research Conference*, Durham, New Hampshire; 27 July.

Ainsworth, P. B. and Pease, K. (1987) *Police Work.* Leicester: BPS.

Alexander, C. (1999) Police psychological burnout and trauma. In J. M. Violanti and D. Paton (eds.) (1999) *Police Trauma: Psychological Aftermath of Civilian Combat.* Springfield IL: Charles C Thomas.

Anselin, L., Cohen, J., Cook, D., Gorr, W. and Tita, G. (1999) Spatial analyses of crime. In *Measurement and Analysis of Crime and Justice*, Volume 4.

Washington DC: US Department of Justice.

Anshel, M. H. (2000) A conceptual model and implications for coping with stressful events in police work. *Criminal Justice and Behaviour*, 27(3), 375–400.

Aronson, E. (1999) *The Social Animal*. New York: Worth.

Aronson, E., Wilson, T. D. and Akert, R. M. (2002) *Social Psychology* (4th ed.). New Jersey: Prentice-Hall.

Asch, S. (1951) Effects of group pressure on the modification and distortion of judgements. In H. Guetzow (ed.) *Groups, Leadership and Men*. Pittsburgh: Carnegie.

Baldwin, J. (1992) *Videotaping Police Interviews with Suspects: An Evaluation*. London: Home Office.

Bandura, A. (1986) *Social Foundations of Thought and Action: A Social Cognitive Theory*. New Jersey: Prentice Hall.

Bandura, A. (1973) *Aggression: A Social Learning Analysis*. New Jersey: Prentice Hall.

Baron, R. A. and Byrne, D. (2000) *Social Psychology* (9th ed.). Boston: Allyn & Bacon.

Bartol, C. R. (1996) Police psychology then, now and beyond. *Criminal Justice and Behaviour*, 23, 70–89.

Belson, W. A. (1979) *Television Violence and the Adolescent Boy*. London: Saxon House.

Ben-Shakhar, G. and Furedy, J. J. (eds.) (1990) *Theories and Applications in the Detection of Deception*. New York: Springer-Verlag.

Bennett, T. (1995) Identifying, explaining and targeting burglary hot spots. *European Journal of Criminal Policy and Research*, 13, 113–123.

Bennett, T. and Wright, R. (1984) *Burglars on Burglary: Prevention and the Offender*. Aldershot: Gower.

Bergen, G. T., Aceto, R. T. and Chadziewicz, M. M. (1992) Job satisfaction of police psychologists. *Criminal Justice and Behaviour*, 19, 314–329.

Berkowitz, L. (1989) The frustration aggression hypothesis: An examination and reformulation. *Psychological Bulletin*, 106, 59–74.

Biggam, F. H., Power, K. G., McDonald, R. R., Carcary, W. B. and Moodie, E. (1997) Self perceived occupational stress and distress in a Scottish police force. *Work and Stress*, 11(2), 118–133.

Blau, T. H. (1994) *Psychological Services for Law Enforcement*. New York: Wiley.

Bohl, N. (1995) Professionally administered critical incident debriefing for police officers. In M. I. Jurke and E. M. Scrivner (eds.) *Police Psychology into the 21st Century*. Hillsdale NJ: LEA.

Borum, W. R. (1988) A comparative study of negotiator effectiveness with 'mentally disturbed hostage-taker' scenarios. *Journal of Police and Criminal Psychology*, 4, 17–20.

Britton, P. (2000) *Picking up the Pieces*. London: Bantam Press.

Brown, J. (2000a) *Gender and Policing: Comparative Perspectives*. Basingstoke: MacMillan.

Brown, J. (2000b) Occupational culture as a factor in the stress experience of police officers. In F. Leishman, B. Loveday and S. Savage (eds.)

Core Issues in Policing (2nd ed.). Harlow: Longman.

Brown, J., Cooper, C. and Kirkcaldy, B. (1996) Occupational stress among senior police officers. *British Journal of Psychology*, 87(1), 31–41.

Brown, R. (1986) *Social Psychology* (2nd ed.). New York: Free Press.

Brown, R. and McNeil, D. (1966). The 'tip-of-the-tongue' phenomenon. *Journal of Verbal Learning and Behavior*, 5, 325–337.

Bull, R. and Horncastle, P. (1988) Evaluating training: The London Metropolitan Police's recruit training in human awareness/policing skills. In P. Southgate (ed.) *New Directions in Police Training*. London: HMSO.

Bull, R. and McAlpine, S. (1998) Facial appearance and criminality. In A. Memon, A. Vrij and R. Bull, *Psychology and Law: Truthfulness, Accuracy and Credibility*. Maidenhead: McGraw-Hill.

Buss, D. M., and Kendrick, D. T. (1998) Evolutionary social psychology. In D. T. Gilbert, S. T. Fiske and G. Lindzey (eds.) *The Handbook of Social Psychology*. New York: McGraw-Hill.

Butler, W. M., Leitenbeg, H. and Fuselier, D.G. (1993) The use of mental health professional consultants to police hostage negotiation teams. *Behavioral Sciences and Law*, 11, 213–221.

Canter, D. and Alison, L. (eds.) (1999) *Profiling in Policy and Practice*. Aldershot: Ashgate.

Canter, D. and Heritage, R. (1990) A multi-variate model of sexual offence behaviour. *Journal of Forensic Psychiatry*, 1(2), 185–212.

Canter, D. and Larkin, P. (1993) The environmental range of serial rapists. *Journal of Environmental Psychology*, 13, 63–69.

Cassell, P. G. (1998) Protecting the innocent from false confessions and lost confessions – and from Miranda. *The Journal of Criminal Law & Criminology*, 88, 497–556.

Chen, P. Y. and Spector, P. E. (1992) Relationships of work stressors with aggression, withdrawal, theft and substance abuse: an exploratory study. *Journal of Occupational and Organizational Psychology*, 65, 177–184.

Cherryman, J. and Bull, R. (2000) Reflections on investigative interviewing. In F. Leishman, B. Loveday and S. Savage (eds.) *Core Issues in Policing* (2nd ed.). Harlow: Longman.

Cialdini, R. B., Vincent, L. E., Lewis, S. K. Catalan, J., Wheeler, D. and Darby, B. L. (1975) Reciprocal concessions procedure for inducing compliance: The door in the face technique. *Journal of Personality and Social Psychology*. 31, 206–215.

Clarke, C. and Milne, R. (2001) *National Evaluation of the PEACE Investigative Interviewing Course*. London: Police Research Award Scheme, Report No. PRAS/149.

Clarke, R. V. (1992) *Situational Crime Prevention: Successful Case Studies*. Albany NY: Harrow & Heston.

Clarke, R. V. (1983) Situational crime prevention: Its theoretical basis and practical scope. In M. Tonry and N. Morris (eds.) *Crime and Justice: An Annual Review of Research, Vol. 4*. Chicago: University of Chicago Press.

Cochrane, R. (1991) Racial prejudice. In R. Cochrane (ed.) *Psychology and Social Issues: A Tutorial Text*. London: Falmer.

Cohen, L. and Felson, M. (1979) Social change and crime rate trends: A routine activity approach. *American Sociological Review*, 44, 588–608.

Cohen, S., Tyrell, D. A. and Smith, A. P. (1991) Psychological stress in humans and susceptibility to the common cold. *New England Journal of Medicine, 325,* 606–612.

Cooper, C. L., Dewe, P. J. and Driscoll, M. P. (2001) *Organisational Stress: A Review and Critique of Theory, Research & Applications*. London: Sage.

Crick, N. R. and Dodge, K. A. (1996) Social information-processing mechanisms in reactive and proactive aggression. *Child Development*, 67, 993–1002.

Croft, S. (1995) Helping victims to remember. *Police*, November: 13–14.

Cutler, B. L. and Penrod, S. D. (1995) *Mistaken Identification: The Eyewitness, Psychology and the Law*. Cambridge: Cambridge University Press.

Davies, A. and Dale, A. (1995) *Locating the Stranger Rapist*. Police Research Group Special Interest Paper 3. London: Home Office Police Department.

Dollard, J., Doob, L. W., Miller, N. E., Mowrer, L. H. and Sears, R. R. (1939) *Frustration and Aggression*. New Haven CT: Yale University Press.

Douglas, J. and Olshaker, M. (1995) *Mindhunter: Inside the FBI Elite Serial Crime Unit*. New York: Scribener.

Downs *v* U.S. (1975) Citation No. 74-1660. U.S. Courts of Appeal, 6th Circ.

Duncan, B. L. (1976) Different social perceptions and attribution of intergroup violence: Testing the lower limits of stereotyping of blacks. *Journal of Personality and Social Psychology*, 34, 590–598.

Dunnette, N. and Motowidlo, S. (1976) *Police Selection and Career Assessment*. Washington DC: US Department of Justice.

Earnshaw, J. and Cooper, C. L. (2001) *Stress and Employer Liability*. London: CIPD.

Ede, R. and Shepherd, E. (1997) *Active Defence: A solicitor's guide to police and defence investigation and prosecution and defence disclosure in criminal cases*. London: The Law Society.

Ekman, P. and O'Sullivan, M. (1991) Who can catch a liar? *American Psychologist*, 46, 913–920.

Ekamn, P., O'Sullivan, M. and Frank, M. G. (1999) A few can catch a liar. *Psychological Science*, 10, 263–266.

Eysenck, M. W. (2001) *Principles of Cognitive Psychology* (2nd ed.). Hove: Psychology Press Ltd.

Eysenck, H. J. (1964) *Crime and Personality*. London: Routledge.

Farber, E. W. and Burge-Callaway, K. (1998) Differences in anger, hostility and interpersonal aggression in Type A and Type B adolescents. *Journal of Clinical Psychology, 54,* 945–952.

Farkas, G. (1986) Stress in undercover policing. In J. Reese and H. Goldstein (eds.) *Psychological Services for Law Enforcement*. Washington DC: US

Government Printing Office.

Farrell, G. and Pease, K. (1993) *Once Bitten Twice Bitten: Repeat Victimization and its Implications for Crime Prevention*. Crime Prevention Unit Paper 46. London: Home Office.

FBI (1995) *Negotiator Notes: Supplemental Training and Administrative Information*. Washington DC: U.S. Department of Justice.

Festinger, L. (1954) A theory of social comparison processes. *Human Relations*, 7, 117–140.

Fisher, R. P., Geiselman, R. E., Raymond, R. S., Jurkevitch, L. M. and Warhaftig, M. L. (1987) Enhancing enhanced eyewitness memory: Refining the cognitive interview. *Journal of Police Science and Administration*, 15, 291–297.

Fitzsimmons, E. (1986) NYPD psychological screening of police candidates: The screening process, issues, and criteria in rejection. In J. Reese and H. Goldstein (eds.) *Psychological Services for Law Enforcement*. Washington DC: US Government Printing Office.

Folkman, S. and Moscowitz, J. T. (2000) The context matters. *Personality and Social Psychology Bulletin*, 26, 150–151.

Foster, J. (1998) Submission to the Home Affairs Select Committee: report on police training and recruitment. Cambridge: Institute of Criminology.

Freedman, J. and Fraser, S. (1966) Compliance without pressure: The foot-in-the-door technique. *Journal of Personality and Social Psychology*, 4, 195–202.

Freud, S. (1930) Why war? In P. Reiff (ed.) *Freud: Character and Culture*. New York: Collier Books.

Frijda, N. H. (1994) The lex Talionis: on vengeance. In S. H. M. Van Goozen, N. A. Van de Poll and J. A. Sergeant (eds.) *Emotions: Essays on Emotion Theory*. New Jersey: Erlbaum.

Geen, R. G. (2001) *Human Aggression* (2nd ed.). Buckingham: Open University Press.

Geiselman, R. E., Fisher, R. P., Cohen, G., Holland, H. and Surtees, L. (1986) Eyewitness responses to leading and misleading questions under the cognitive interview. *Journal of Police Science and Administration*, 14, 31–39.

Geller, W. A. and Toch, H. (1996) *Police Violence: Understanding and Controlling Police Abuse of Force*. New Haven: Yale University Press.

George, R. C. (1991) A field evaluation of the Cognitive Interview. Unpublished M.A. thesis, Polytechnic of East London.

Getty, V. and Elam, J. (1988) Identifying characteristics of hostage negotiators and using personality data to develop a selection model. In J. Reese and H. Goldstein (eds.) *Police Psychology: Operational Assistance*. Washington DC: US Department of Justice.

Gilbert, D. T., McNulty, S. E., Giuliano, T. A. and Benson, J. E. (1992) Blurry words and fuzzy deeds: The attribution of obscure behaviour. *Journal of Personality and Social Psychology*, 62, 18–25.

Gluek, S. and Gluek, E. T. (1956) *Physique and Delinquency*. New York: Dodd Meade.

Gowan, M. A. and Gatewood, R. D. (1995) Personnel selection. In N. Brewer and C. Wilson (eds.) *Psychology and Policing*. Hillsdale, USA: Lawrence Erlbaum Associates.

Granhag, P. A. and Stromwall, L. A. (2001) Deception detection based on repeated interrogations. *Legal and Criminological Psychology*, 6, 85–101.

Gregory, R. L. (1980) Perceptions as hypotheses. *Philosophical Translations of the Royal Society of London, Series B*, 290, 181–197.

Gudjonsson, G. H. (2001) False confession. *The Psychologist*, 14(11), 588–591.

Gudjonsson, G. H. (1992*) The Psychology of Interrogations, Confessions and Testimony*. Chichester: Wiley.

Gudjonsson, G. H. (1991) Suggestibility and compliance among alleged false confessors and resisters in criminal trials. *Medicine, Science and the Law*, 31, 147–151.

Gudjonsson, G. H. and Clark, N. K. (1986) Suggestibility in police interrogation: A social psychological model. *Social Behavior*, 1, 83–104.

Gudjonsson, G. H. and Haward, L. R. C. (1998*) Forensic Psychology: A Guide to Practice*. London: Routledge.

Gudjonsson, G. H. and MacKeith, J. A. C. (1982) False confessions: Psychological effects of interrogation. In A. Trankell (ed.) *Reconstructing the Past*. Deventer: Kluwer.

Gudjonsson. G. H. and Sigurdsson, J. F. (1994) How frequently do false confessions occur? An empirical study among prison inmates. *Psychology, Crime and Law*, 1, 21–26.

Hall, D. F., Loftus, E. F., and Tousignant, J. P. (1984) Postevent information and changes in recollection for a natural event. In G. L. Wells and E. F. Loftus (eds.) *Eyewitness Testimony: Psychological Perspectives*. New York: Cambridge University Press.

Hammer, J. and Griffiths, S. (2000) *Reducing Domestic Violence... What Works? Policing Domestic Violence*. PRCU Crime Reduction Research Series. London: Home Office.

Hatcher, C., Mohandie, K., Turner, J. and Gelles, M. G. (1998) The role of the psychologist in crisis/hostage negotiations. *Behavioral Sciences and the Law*, 16, 455–472.

Hazelwood, R. R. (1987) Analyzing the rape and profiling the offender. In R. R. Hazelwood and A. W. Burgess (eds.) *Practical Aspects of Rape Investigation: A Multidisciplinary Approach*. New York: Elsevier.

Heider, F. (1958) *The Psychology of Interpersonal Relations*. New York: Harper.

Hibler, N. S. and Kurke, M. I. (1995) Ensuring personal reliability through selection and training. In M. I. Jurke and E. M. Scrivner (eds.) *Police Psychology into the 21st Century*. Hillsdale NJ: LEA.

Higginbotham, J. (1994) Legal issues in crisis management. *FBI Law Enforcement Bulletin*, 63, 27–32.

Hobbes, T. (1651/1978) *The Leviathan*. Harmondsworth: Penguin.

Holmes, T. H. and Rahe, R. H. (1967) The social readjustment rating scale. *Journal of Psychosomatic Medicine*, 11, 213–218.

Hough, M., Clarke, R. V. and Mayhew, P. (1980) Introduction in R.V. Clarke and P. Mayhew (eds.) *Designing Out Crime*. London: HMSO.

Inbau, F. E. and Reid, J. F. (1963) *Criminal Interrogation and Confessions*. Toronto: Burns & MacEachern.

Inbau, F. E., Reid, J. E. and Buckley, P. (1986*) Criminal Interrogation and Confession*. (3rd ed.). Baltimore MD: Williams & Wilkins.

Jackson, J. L., Van Den Eshof, P. and de Kluever, E. E. (1997) A research approach to offender profiling. In J. L. Jackson and D. A. Bekerian (eds.) *Offender Profiling: Theory, Research and Practice*. Chichester: Wiley.

Kassin, S. M. and Sukel, H. (1997) Coerced confessions and the jury: An experimental test of the 'harmless error' rule. *Law and Human Behavior*, 21, 27–46.

Kebbell, M., Milne, R. and Wagstaff, G, (1999) The cognitive interview: A survey of its forensic effectiveness. *Psychology, Crime & Law*, 5, 101–116.

Kebbell, M. R. and Wagstaff, G. F. (1999*) Face Value? Evaluating the Accuracy of Eyewitness Information*. Police Research Series Paper 102. London: Home Office.

Kelly, H. H. (1967) Attribution theory in social psychology. In D. Levine (ed.) *Nebraska Symposium on Motivation (Vol. 15)*. Lincoln: University of Nebraska Press.

Kemshall, H. and Pritchard, J. (1999) (eds.) *Good Practice in Working with Violence*. London: Jessica Kingsley.

Kendall, D., McElroy, H., and Dale, A. (1999) Developments in offender profiling: The analysis of rapists' speech. *Police Research and Management, 3(3)*, 69–80.

Klockars, C.B. (1996) A theory of excessive force and its control. In W. A. Geller and H. Toch. *Police Violence: Understanding and Controlling Police Abuse of Force*. New Haven: Yale University Press.

Kohnken, G., Milne, R., Memon, A. and Bull, R. (1999) The cognitive interview: A meta-analysis. *Psychology, Crime and Law*, 5, 3–28.

Kurke, M. I. and Scrivner, E. M. (eds.) (1995) *Police Psychology into the 21st Century*. Hillsdale NJ: LEA.

Lefkowitz, J. (1977) Industrial-organisational psychology and the police. *American Psychologist*, 32 (5) 346–364.

Leng, R. (1994) The right to silence debate. In D. Morgan and G. Stephenson (eds.) *Suspicion and Silence: The Right to Silence in Criminal Investigations*. London: Blackstone.

Leo, R. A. (1996) Inside the interrogation room. *The Journal of Criminal Law and Criminology*, 86, 266–303.

Levelt, W. J. M., Roelofs, A. and Meyer, A. S. (1999) A theory of lexical access in speech production. *Behavioral and Brain Sciences*, 22, 1–38.

Lipton, J. P. (1977) On the psychology of eyewitness testimony. *Journal of Applied Psychology*, 62, 90–93.

Loftus, E. F. (2001) Imagining the past. *The Psychologist*, 14(11) 584–587.

Loftus, E. F. (1979) *Eyewitness Testimony*. Cambridge, Mass: Harvard University Press.

Loftus, E. F. (1977) Shifting human color memory. *Memory and Cognition, 5*, 696–699.

Loftus, E. F. (1975) Leading questions and the eyewitness report. *Cognitive Psychology*, 7, 560–572.

Loftus, E. F. and Greene, E. (1980) Warning: Even memories for faces can be contagious. *Law and Human Behavior, 4*, 323–334.

Loftus, E. F., Loftus, G. R. and Messo, J. (1987) Some facts about weapon focus. *Law and Human Behaviour, 11*, 55–62.

Loftus, E. F., Miller, D. G. and Burns, H. J. (1978) Semantic integration of verbal information into visual memory. *Journal of Experimental Psychology (Human Learning and Memory), 4*, 19–31.

Loftus, E. F. and Palmer, J. C. (1974) Reconstructions of automobile destruction: an example of the interaction between language and memory. *Journal of Verbal Learning and Verbal Behavior, 13*, 585–589.

Lore, R. K. and Schultz, L. A. (1993) Control of human aggression: A comparative perspective. *American Psychologist, 48*, 16–25.

Lorenz, K. (1966) *On Aggression*. New York: Harcourt.

MacPherson, Sir William of Cluny (1999) *The Stephen Lawrence Inquiry*. Cmnd. 4262–1. London: HMSO.

Mayhew, P., Clarke, R. V., Sturman, A. and Hough, J. M. (1976) *Crime as Opportunity*. Home Office Research Study No. 34. London: HMSO

McCann, J. T. (1998) A conceptual framework for identifying various types of confessions. *Behavioral Sciences and the Law*, 16, 441–453.

McConkey, K. M. and Sheehan, P. W. (1995) *Hypnosis, Memory and Behaviour in Criminal Investigation*. New York: Guildford Press.

McConville, M. and Hodgson, J. (1993) *Custodial Legal Advice and the Right to Silence*. London: HMSO.

McMains, M. J. (1988) Psychologist's roles in hostage negotiations. In J. Reese and J. Horn (eds.) *Police Psychology: Operational Assistance*. Washington DC: Federal Bureau of Investigation.

McMains, M., and Mullins, W. C. (1996) *Crisis Negotiations: Managing Critical Incidents and Situations in Law Enforcement and Corrections*. Cincinnati OH: Anderson.

Milgram, S. (1965) Some conditions of obedience and disobedience to authority. *Human Relations*, 18, 57–76.

Milne, R. and Bull, R. (1999) *Investigative Interviewing: Psychology and Practice*. Chichester: Wiley.

Miller, J. G. (1984) Culture and the development of everyday social explanation. *Journal of Personality and Social Psychology*, 46, 961–978.

Mirrlees-Black, C., Budd, C., Partridge, S. and Mayhew, P. (1998) *The 1998 British Crime Survey, England & Wales*. Home Office Statistical Bulletin 21/98. London: Home Office.

Moston, S., Stephenson, G. M. and Williamson, T.M. (1992) The effects of case characteristics on suspect behaviour during police questioning. *British Journal of Criminology*, 92, 23–40.

National Crime Faculty (1996) *Investigate Interviewing: A Practical Guide*. Bramshill: National Crime Faculty and National Police Training.

Neisser, U. (1967) *Cognitive Psychology*. New York: Appleton-Century Crofts.

Noesner, G. and Nolan, J. (1992) First responder negotiation training. *FBI Law Enforcement Bulletin*, 61(8), 1–4.

Novaco, R. W. (1991) Aggression on roadways. In R. Baenninger (ed.) *Targets of Violence and Aggression*. Amsterdam: Elsevier.

Ofshe, R. (1989) Coerced confessions: The logic of seemingly irrational action. *Cultic Studies Journal*, 6, 1–15.

Orne, M. (1984) Hypnotically induced testimony. In G. L. Wells, and E. F. Loftus (eds.) *Eyewitness Testimony: Psychological Perspectives*. New York: Cambridge University Press.

Oxford, T. (1991) Spotting a Liar. *Police Review*, 328–329.

Parent, R. B. and Verdun-Jones, S. (2000) When police kill: the aftermath. *The Police Journal, 73(3)*, 241–255.

Park, B. and Kraus, S. (1992) Consensus in initial impressions as a function of verbal information. *Personality and Social Psychology Bulletin, 18*, 439–446.

Parker, A. D. and Brown, J. (2000) Detection of deception: Statement validity assessment as a means of determining truthfulness or falsity of rape allegations. *Legal and Criminological Psychology*, 5(2), 237–260.

Pease, K. (1998) *Repeat Victimization: Taking Stock*. Crime Prevention and Detection Series, Paper 90. London: Home Office Police Research Group.

Pease, K. (1996) *Repeat Victimization and Policing*. Unpublished manuscript, University of Huddersfield.

Peay, J. (1997) Mentally disordered offenders. In M. Maguire, R. Morgan and R. Reiner (eds.) *The Oxford Handbook of Criminology* (2nd ed.). Oxford: Oxford University Press.

Pickel, K. L. (1998) Unusualness and threat as possible causes of weapon focus. *Memory, 6*, 277–295.

Rand Corporation (1975) *The Criminal Investigation Process, Volumes 1–3*. Santa Monica CA: Rand Corporation.

Rattner, A. (1998) Convicted but innocent: Wrongful conviction and the criminal justice system. *Law and Human Behavior*, 12, 283–293.

Reisser, M. (1995) Foreword in M. I. Kurke and E. M. Scrivner (eds.) *Police Psychology into the 21st Century*. Hillsdale NJ: LEA.

Reisser, M. (1989) Investigative hypnosis. In D. C. Raskin (ed.) *Psychological Methods in Criminal Investigation and Evidence*. New York: Springer.

Richmond, R. L., Kehoe, L., Hailstone, S., Wodal, A. and Ubelm Y. M. (1999) Quantitative and qualitative evaluation of brief interventions to change excessive drinking, smoking and stress in the police force. *Addiction, 94(10)*, 1509–1521.

Ross, L. (1977) The intuitive psychologist and his shortcomings: Distortions in the attribution process. In L. Berkowitz (ed.) *Advances in Experimental Social Psychology (Vol. 10)*. New York: Academic Press.

Rossmo, D. K. (1997) Geographic profiling. In J. L. Jackson and D. A. Bekerian (eds.) *Offender Profiling*. Chichester: Wiley.

Rossmo, D. K. (1996) Targeting victims: serial killers and the urban environment. In T. O'Reilly-Fleming (ed.) *Serial and Mass Murder: Theory, Research and Policy*. Toronto: Canadian Scholars Press.

Rotter, J. B. (1966) Generalised expectancies for internal versus external control of reinforcement. *Psychological Monographs, 80* (1, whole no. 609).

Sanders, G. S. (1986) *The Usefulness of Eyewitness Research from the Perspective of Police Investigators*. Unpublished manuscript, State University of New York.

Scarman, Rt. Hon. Lord (1981) The Brixton disorders 10–12th April 1981: *Report of an Enquiry by the Rt. Hon. Lord Scarman*. Cmnd 8247. London: HMSO.

Schmidt, F. L. and Hunter, J. E. (1998) The validity and utility of selection models in personnel psychology: Practical and theoretical implications of 85 years of research findings. *Psychological Bulletin*, 124(2) 262–274.

Schonborn, K. (2001) *Policing Society: A Comparative Look at Violence, the Use of Force and Other Issues in the US and the UK*. Duboque, Iowa: Kendall/Hunt.

Scott, J. P. (1958) *Aggression*. Chicago: University of Chicago Press.

Sear, L. and Williamson, T. (1999) British and American interrogation strategies. In D. Canter and L. Alison (eds.) *Interviewing and Deception*. Aldershot: Ashgate.

Selye, H. (1956) *The Stress of Life*. New York: McGraw-Hill.

Sewell, J. D. (1983) The development of a critical life events scale for law enforcement. *Journal of Police Science and Administration, 11 (1)*, 113–114.

Shepherd, E. (1993) Resistance in interviews: The contribution of police perceptions and behaviour. In E. Shepherd (ed.) *Aspects of Police Interviewing*. Leicester: British Psychological Society.

Shipherd, J. C. and Beck, J. G. (1999) The effects of suppressing trauma-related thoughts on women with rape-related PTSD. *Behavior Research and Therapy*, 37, 99–112.

Shusman, E. and Inwald, R. (1991) A longtitudinal validation study of correctional officer job performance as predicted by the IPI and the MMPI. *Journal of Criminal Justice*, 19(4), 173–180.

Slatkin, A. A. (1998) The Stockholm Syndrome and situational factors related to its development. *Dissertation Abstracts International*, 58(7-B) Jan 1998. 3970, US.

Sommer, R. (1969) *Personal Space*. New Jersey: Prentice Hall.

Stone, V. and Tuffin, R. (2000) *Attitudes of People from Minority Ethnic Communities Towards a Career in the Police Service*. Police Research Series Paper 136. London: Home Office.

Steblay, N. M. (1992) A meta-analytic review of the weapon focus effect.

Law and Human Behavior, 16, 413–424.

Stewart, J. K. (1985) Cited in R. E. Geiselman *Interviewing Victims and Witnesses of Crime*. US Department of Justice, Washington DC: Research in Brief. December.

Storr, A. (1970) *Human Aggression*. New York: Bantam Books.

Strentz, T. (1979) Law enforcement policy and ego defenses of hostages. *FBI Law Enforcement Bulletin*, 8, 2–12.

Super, J. T. (1999) Forensic psychology and law enforcement. In A. K. Hess and I. B. Weiner (eds.) *The Handbook of Forensic Psychology* (2nd ed). New York: Wiley.

Swanson, C. R., Chamelin, N. C. and Territon. L. (1988) *Criminal Investigation* (4th ed.). New York: McGraw-Hill.

Tabol, C. E. and Ainsworth, P. B. (2000) Role conflict and role ambiguity amongst a sample of British police officers; implications for psychological well-being. Paper presented to the 10th European Conference of Psychology and Law, Cyprus: April.

Tajfel, H. (1971) Social categorisation and inter-group behaviour. *European Journal of Social Psychology*, 1, 149–178.

Taylor, S. E., Peplau, A. A. and Sears, D. O. (2000) *Social Psychology* (10th ed.). New Jersey: Prentice Hall.

Terman, L. M. and Otis, A. (1917) A trial of mental and pedagogical tests in civil servant examination for policemen and firemen. *Journal of Applied Psychology*, 1, 17—29.

Tesser, A. and Beach, S. R. H. (1998) Life events, relationship quality and depression: An investigation of judgement discontinuity in vivo. *Journal of Personality and Social Psychology*, 74, 36–52.

Thomas-Riddle, F. R. (2000) The relationship between life stress, work stress, and traumatic stress and burnout and cynicism in police officers. *Dissertation Abstracts International*, 60(9-B).

Toch, H. (2002) *Stress in Policing*. Washington DC: American Psychological Association.

Vila, G., Porche, L. M., and Mouren-Simeoni, M. (1999) An 18-month longitudinal study of PTSD in children who were taken hostage in their school. *Psychosomatic Medicine*, 61(6), 746–754.

Vrij, A. (2001) Detecting the liars. *The Psychologist*, 14(11), 596–598.

Vrij, A. (2000) *Detecting Lies and Deceit: The Psychology of Lying and the Implications for Professional Practice*. Chichester: Wiley.

Vrij, A. and Semin, G.R. (1996) Lie experts' belief about nonverbal indicators of deception. *Journal of Nonverbal Behavior*, 20, 65–80.

Wagstaff, G. F. (1993) What expert witnesses can tell courts about hypnosis: A review of the association between hypnosis and the law. *British Journal of Experimental and Clinical Hypnosis*, 2, 3–12.

Wakefield, H. and Underwager, R. (1998) Coerced and nonvoluntary confessions. *Behavioral Sciences & the Law*, 16 (4), 423–440.

Weingardt, K. R., Toland, H. K., and Loftus, E. F. (1994) Reports of suggested memories: Do people truly believe them? In D. F. Ross, J. D. Read and M. P. Toglia (eds.) *Adult Eyewitness Testimony: Current Trends and Developments*. Cambridge: Cambridge University Press.

Wellbrook, K. D. (2000) Stress, hardiness, social support network orientation and trauma-related symptoms in police officers. *Dissertation Abstracts International, 61(3-B)*.

Wells, G. L., Small, M., Penrod, S. D., Malpass, R. S., Fulero, S. M. and Brimacombe, C. A. E. (1998) Eyewitness identification procedures: Recommendations for lineups and photospreads. *Law & Human Behavior, 22*, 603–645.

Westmorland, L. (2001) *Gender and Policing*. Cullompton: Willan.

White, E. K. and Honig, A. L. (1995) The role of the police psychologist in training. In M. I. Jurke and E. M. Scrivner (eds.) *Police Psychology into the 21st Century*. Hillsdale NJ: LEA.

Wiles, P. and Costello, A. (2000) *The Road to Nowhere: The Evidence for Travelling Criminals*. Home Office Briefing Note No. 4/00. London: Policing and Reducing Crime Unit.

Williamson, T. (1994) Reflections on current police practice. In D. Morgan and G. Stephenson (eds.) *Suspicion and Silence: The Right to Silence in Criminal Investigations*. London: Blackstone Press.

Wilson, M. and Smith, A. (2000) Rules and roles in terrorist hostage taking. In D. Canter, and L. Alison (eds.) *The Social Psychology of Crime: Groups, Teams and Networks*. Aldershot: Ashgate.

Wilson, P., Lincoln, R. and Koscis, R. (1997) Validity, utility and ethics of profiling for serial violent and sexual offences. *Psychiatry, Psychology and Law, 4*, 1–11.

Wright, D. B., Self, G. and Justice, C. (2000) Memory conformity: Exploring misinformation effects when presented by another person. *British Journal of Psychology*, 91(2), 189–202.

Zimbardo, P. (1966) The psychology of imprisonment. In J. C. Brigham and L. S. Wrightsman (eds.) *Contemporary Issues in Social Psychology*. Belmont, CA: Brookes/Cole.

Index